FRESH & TASTY

Mainly
vegetables

R&R PUBLICATIONS MARKETING PTY LTD

Published by:
R&R Publications Marketing Pty. Ltd
ACN 083 612 579
PO Box 254, Carlton North, Victoria 3054 Australia
Phone (61 3) 9381 2199 Fax (61 3) 9381 2689
Australia wide toll free 1800 063 296
E-mail: richardc@bigpond.net.au

©Richard Carroll

Fresh & Tasty Mainly Vegetables

Publisher: Richard Carroll
Creative Director: Lucy Adams
Production Manager: Anthony Carroll
Food Photography: Steve Baxter, Phillip Wilkins, David Munns, Thomas Odulate, Christine Hanscomb
and Frank Wieder
Home Economist: Sara Buenfeld, Emma Patmore, Nancy McDougall, Louise Pickford, Oded Schwartz,
Alison Austin and Jane Lawrie
Food Stylists: Helen Payne, Sue Russell, Sam Scott, Antonia Gaunt and Oded Schwartz
Recipe Development: Terry Farris, Jacqueline Bellefontaine, Becky Johnson, Valerie Barrett, Emma
Patmore, Geri Richards, Pam Mallender and Jan Fullwood
Nutritional Consultant: Moya de Wet BSc SRD
Proof Reader: Paul Hassing

Includes Index
ISBN 1 74022 228 8
EAN 9 781740 222 280

First Edition Printed September 2002
Computer Typeset in Adobe Garamond
Printed in Singapore

Contents

Introduction

Vegetarian eating is a healthy alternative for today's lifestyle. Meals without meat, poultry or seafood are attractive, tasty and satisfying - as well as being good for you. The recipes in this book provide delectable dishes which can be combined or enjoyed as a hearty meal on their own. Influenced by cuisines from around the world, there are easy-to-prepare dishes which have the wonderful texture and flavor of fresh vegetables, raw and cooked.

From an Asian-influenced soup to scrumptious desserts, this selection of satisfying and delicious recipes will enable you to prepare natural healthy food for every appetite and occasion, from a quick snack to a 3-course dinner party.

Vegetable Know-How
To make the most of your garden-fresh vegetables, we've put together these essential step-by-step preparation and cooking tips.

Ready
Easy preparation and cooking depends on having a few good basic pieces of equipment. To make life easier, it's worth investing in such as a large chopping board, a small sharp vegetable or paring knife, as several larger sharp knives for cutting and chopping, a grater, a vegetable peeler and a colander or large sieve. Remember to keep your knives sharp: either learn to sharpen them yourself or take them to a knife sharpener regularly. Sharp knives make preparation a breeze.

Set
Wash vegetables before preparing, but do not soak. Soaking tends to draw out the valuable water-soluble vitamins and you end up with vegetables with a lower nutrient content.
If you do find it necessary to soak very dirty vegetables to remove grime and creepy-crawlies, keep the soaking time to a minimum.

- Vegetables left whole with their skins on have a higher nutrient and fiber content than those that are finely chopped and peeled. Many of the precious vitamins and minerals in vegetables are stored just under the skin, so only peel vegetables if necessary.
- For maximum nutritional value, prepare vegetables just before cooking and serve them as soon as they're are cooked.
- The smaller the portion, the quicker the cooking time. For example, grated carrot will cook more quickly than carrot cut into slices.

Go
- To cube, cut into about 1cm/$\frac{1}{2}$in pieces.
- To dice, cut into 5mm/$\frac{1}{4}$in pieces.
- To mince, cut into 2$\frac{1}{4}$mm/$\frac{1}{8}$in pieces.
- To grate, use either a hand grater or a food processor with a grating attachment.
- To slice, cut from very thin to thick. You can also slice into rings. Another way to slice is to cut diagonally. This is a good way to prepare vegetables such as carrots, celery and zucchini for stir-frying.

Remember the three Ms
- Minimum water.
- Minimum cooking.
- Minimum cutting.

Good for You
Health authorities recommend that we eat 4 serves of vegetables daily, at least 1 of which should be raw. The old adage of a white, a yellow and a green may be rarely taught these days, but it's a good reminder that brightly coloured vegetables are usually the best source of vitamins.

Pantry Planning

Try the following tips for no-fuss pantry planning.

- If you store herbs and spices in alphabetical order, they are easily located and you can see when they need replacing.
- Growing a few herbs of your own such as basil, cilantro, rosemary, mint, chives and parsley means you always have these on hand. Fresh herbs are often the secret to delicate flavors in meals.
- Place all staples, such as sugar and flour together. Store sauces and condiments according to your favourite cuisines; just a glance in the cupboard will give you great ideas.
- Keep a good selection of frozen vegetables. Peas, beans, spinach and corn are great standbys and only take minutes to cook in the microwave.
- Keep a variety of breads and rolls in the freezer and defrost in the microwave for delicious instant sandwiches.
- Cooked pasta and rice freeze well; reheat in minutes in the microwave and save time on busy nights.
- Evaporated milk, available as full-cream or skim milk, is a terrific standby when there is no fresh cream. It can be used for sauces and quiches and it whips well when chilled. Store a few cans in the pantry for emergencies.

Fibre in Vegetables

Vegetable	Serve	Fibre*
Asparagus, boiled	6–8 spears(55g/2oz)	1.4g
Beans, green, raw	1/2 cup (6g/1/6 oz)	1.2g
Bean sprouts	2 tablespoons (10g/1/3 oz)	0.3g
Beetroot, canned	2 slices (20g/2/3 oz)	0.6g
Broccoli, boiled	2/3 cup (100g/31/2 oz)	3.9g
Cabbage, white, boiled	1/2 cup (6g/1/6 oz)	1.0g
Zucchini, boiled	1 medium (110g/33/4 oz)	1.5g
Bell pepper, green, raw	1/4 cup (40g/11/3 oz)	0.5g
Carrot, peeled, boiled	1 carrot (100g/31/2 oz)	2.9g
Cauliflower, boiled	2/3 cup (100g/31/2 oz)	2.0g
Celery, raw	1 stalk (100g/31/2 oz)	0.8g
Chili, raw	2 chilies (6g/1/6 oz)	0.6g
Corn	1/2 cup kernels (75g/21/2 oz)	3.5g
Cucumber, peeled, raw	4–5 slices (20g/2/3 oz)	0.1g
Eggplant, baked	1/2 small (75g/21/2 oz)	2.7g
Garlic, raw	2 cloves (10g/1/3 oz)	1.7g
Leek, boiled	1 leek (6g/1/6 oz)	1.4g
Lettuce, raw	2 leaves (20g/2/3 oz)	0.1g
Mushrooms, fried	4–6 mushrooms (75g/21/2 oz)	1.4g
Olives	3 green (20g/2/3 oz)	0.8g
Onion, peeled, fried	1 onion (80g/23/4 oz)	2.2g
Parsley	2 sprigs (2g/1/12 oz)	0.1g
Peas, green, boiled	1/3 cup (40g/11/3 oz)	1.0g
Potato, peeled, roasted	1 medium (120g/41/4 oz)	2.4g
Potato, unpeeled, boiled	1 medium (120g/41/4 oz)	3.0g
Pumpkin, peeled, boiled	1/2 cup (80g/23/4 oz)	2.4g
Radish, red, raw	2 radishes (10g/1/3 oz)	0.1g
Silverbeet, boiled	3 stalks (100g/31/2 oz)	2.1g
Tomato, raw	1 medium (130g/42/3 oz)	2.4g

* grams of dietary fiber per serve.

Left to right:
Cubed, Diced, Minced,
Grated, Sliced

Soups and Starters

Spinach and almond, leek and lime, bean and bread. Soup is the stage where everything goes, and vegetables are versatile players indeed. Curried, creamed or cold, these enchanting liquid delights will ensure your dinners receive rave reviews at every performance. A supporting cast of talented starters is also present in this chapter, ready to fill any role that takes your fancy. So why not start auditions today?

Avocado Gazpazho

Note: On a balmy summer evening, what better start to a meal than this iced gazpacho with its extra avocado? Serve with crusty bread to mop up the last delicious drop!

Serves 4
Preparation 15mins plus 1hr chilling
Calories 206
Fat 18g

**2 large ripe avocados, stoned, peeled and chopped
grated zest and juice of
1 lemon
2¹/₂ cups vegetable stock
2 large tomatoes
1 cucumber, chopped
1 green and 1 red capsicum, deseeded and chopped
1 clove garlic, crushed
salt and black pepper
4 tbsp freshly snipped chives
to garnish**

1 Place the avocados, lemon zest and juice and the stock in a food processor and blend to a thin, smooth purée, or use a hand blender. Pour into a large bowl and set aside.

2 Place the tomatoes in a bowl, cover with boiling water and leave for 30 seconds. Remove from the bowl, peel off the skins, then deseed and chop the flesh. Reserve a little chopped tomato and cucumber to garnish. Place the rest of the tomatoes and cucumber in the food processor with the capsicums, garlic and seasoning, then blend to a purée. Alternatively, use a hand blender.

3 Add the tomato mixture to the avocado purée, mixing thoroughly. Cover and refrigerate for 1 hour, then serve garnished with chives and the reserved tomato and cucumber.

Photograph appears also on page 6

French Vegetable Soup with Pistou

455g/1 lb fresh borlotti or dried navy beans
1 large onion
455g/1 lb green beans
455g/1 lb zucchini or squash
6 medium potatoes
30g/1oz butter
14 cups water
1–2 tsp salt (the amount of vegetables calls for a good seasoning)
55g/2oz farfalle (pasta bows)

Pistou
1 cup basil leaves
4 cloves garlic
1 large tomato
1 tbs tomato paste
$^1/_2$ cup grated Parmesan or Gruyere cheese
3 tbs olive oil

1 If using dried beans, soak overnight.
2 Place the soaked and drained dried beans in a pan with fresh water to cover. Bring to the boil, cover and simmer gently for 15 minutes. Drain.
3 Chop the onion finely. Trim and cut the zucchini or squash into 5mm/$^1/_4$ in slices. Peel the potatoes and cut into 1cm/$^1/_2$ in dice.
4 Melt the butter in a large deep pan and saute the prepared vegetables, including the dried and cooked, or fresh white beans, until softened for about 5 minutes. Cover with cold water and add salt. Cover and simmer gently for 1 hour. Add the farfalle to the soup, cooking for a further 15 minutes.
5 Make pistou by processing the basil with the garlic in a food processor or blender. Peel and chop the tomato and add to the basil with the tomato paste and cheese. Puree to a paste, adding oil gradually.
6 Stir the pistou into the soup just before serving. Serve piping hot with crusty bread.

Serves 4–6
Preparation 30mins
Cooking 40mins
Calories 779
Fat 6g

Spinach and Almond Soup

*Note: Not only do
the almonds add
their distinctive taste
to this spinach soup,
they also give it a
lovely thick texture.
It's delicious hot or
cold - especially if
you use fresh stock.*

455g/1 lb baby spinach
3½ cups vegetable stock
100g/3½ oz ground almonds
salt and black pepper
115mL/4 fl oz single cream
55g Parmesan, grated,
to serve

1 Put the spinach into a large
saucepan with the stock, reserving a
few leaves to garnish. Bring to the
boil, then reduce the heat and
simmer for 5 minutes. Stir in the
almonds and seasoning and simmer
for 2 minutes. Remove from the
heat and leave to cool a little.
2 Pour into a food processor and
blend to a smooth purée, or use a
hand blender. Add the cream,
return to the pan and reheat gently
- don't let the soup boil. Serve
topped with the Parmesan and a
sprinkling of pepper, and garnished
with the reserved spinach.

Serves 4
Preparation 5mins
Cooking 10mins
Calories 291
Fat 24g

Tuscan Bean and Bread Soup

¹/₂ loaf ciabatta bread
3 tbsp olive oil
3 onions, chopped
3 cloves garlic, chopped
2 x 400g/14oz cans
chopped tomatoes
400g/14oz can flageolet beans
2¹/₂ cups vegetable stock
salt and black pepper
fresh basil to garnish

1 Preheat the oven. Cut the ciabatta into dice, then place in the oven for 10 minutes to dry out.
2 Heat the oil in a large saucepan, add the onions and garlic, and cook for 3–4 minutes, until soft. Add the tomatoes, beans and stock, bring to the boil, then simmer for 2 minutes.
3 Stir in the diced ciabatta, bring the soup back to the boil, then simmer for a further 5 minutes. Season, then serve garnished with basil.

OVEN TEMPERATURE
150°C, 300°F, GAS 2

Serves 4
Preparation 10mins
Cooking 20mins
Calories 335
Fat 14g

Leek, Lime and Coconut Soup

Note: The Thai flavours of lime and coconut totally transform this classic leek and potato soup. You can enjoy it hot or cold, depending on your mood and the weather.

Serves 4
Preparation 15mins
Cooking 35mins
Calories 283
Fat 20g

2 tbsp olive oil
3 leeks, thinly sliced
1 green chilli, deseeded and chopped
2 potatoes, diced
grated zest and juice of 2 limes, plus a few extra slices to garnish
salt and black pepper
2¼ cups vegetable stock
1 cup coconut milk
fresh coriander to garnish

1 Heat the oil in a large heavy-based saucepan, then add the leeks, chilli, potatoes, lime zest and seasoning. Cook for 2 minutes, then add the stock and bring to the boil. Reduce the heat and simmer for 20–25 minutes, until the potatoes are tender. Leave to cool slightly.
2 Transfer the soup to a food processor and blend briefly to make a chunky, creamy mixture, or use a hand blender. Return the soup to the pan.
3 Stir in the lime juice, then add the coconut milk and heat through, taking care not to let the soup boil. Serve hot or cold, garnished with slices of lime and the coriander.

Thick Minestrone with Pesto

3 tbsp olive oil
1 onion, chopped
2 cloves garlic, chopped
1 potato, cut into
1cm/^{1}/$_2$ in cubes
2 small carrots, cut into
1cm/^{1}/$_2$ in cubes
1 large zucchini, cut into
1cm/^{1}/$_2$ in cubes
^{1}/$_4$ white cabbage, chopped
3 cups vegetable stock
2 x 400g/14oz cans chopped
tomatoes
85g/3oz pasta shapes, such
as conchiglie shells
salt and black pepper
4 tbsp grated Parmesan
4 tbsp pesto

1 Place the oil in a large heavy-based saucepan, then add the onion, garlic, potato, carrots, zucchini and cabbage and cook for 5–7 minutes, until slightly softened.
2 Add the stock and tomatoes and bring to the boil. Reduce the heat and simmer for 20 minutes, then add the pasta and seasoning and cook for a further 15 minutes or until the pasta is tender but still firm to the bite. Divide the soup between bowls and top each serving with a tablespoon of Parmesan and pesto.

Serves 4
Preparation 20mins
Cooking 45mins
Calories 370
Fat 21g

Curried Cream of Vegetable Soup

Note: A dollop of crème fraîche makes a creamy contrast to the spicy flavour of this versatile soup. Use seasonal vegetables, and serve with warm French bread.

Serves 4
Preparation 20mins
Cooking 30mins
Calories 433
Fat 22g

3 tbsp groundnut or vegetable oil
2 tbsp curry powder
pinch each of ground cinnamon, nutmeg, turmeric and ginger
3 carrots, diced
2 onions, chopped
2 cloves garlic, chopped
2 potatoes, diced
2 zucchinis, diced
4 cups vegetable stock
285g/10oz can cannellini beans, drained
225g/8oz can red kidney beans, drained
200mL/7 fl oz crème fraîche
salt
2 tsp chopped fresh Italian parsley to garnish

1 Place the oil in a large heavy-based saucepan. Add the curry powder, cinnamon, nutmeg, turmeric and ginger and cook for 1 minute, then add the carrots, onions, garlic, potatoes and zucchinis. Stir to coat thoroughly in the oil and spice mixture and cook for a further 5 minutes.

2 Add the stock and bring to the boil. Reduce the heat and simmer for 20 minutes or until the vegetables are tender. Add the cannellini and red kidney beans and gently heat through. Remove from the heat and stir in the crème fraîche. Season to taste and serve sprinkled with the parsley.

Artichokes with Soured Cream Sauce

4 large globe artichokes
salt
285mL/10 fl oz sour cream
5 spring onions, finely chopped
1 tbsp balsamic vinegar
1 clove garlic, finely chopped

1 Cut off the artichoke stalks, so that the artichokes stand flat. Place in a large saucepan of boiling salted water and simmer, partly covered, for 40 minutes or until tender. To test if the artichokes are cooked, pull off an outside leaf - it should come away easily. Remove the artichokes from the pan and set aside for 30 minutes to cool.

2 Meanwhile, make the sauce. Mix together the sour cream, spring onions, vinegar and garlic. Pull the central cone of leaves out of each artichoke, leaving a wall of leaves around the edge, and discard. Scrape away the inedible core with a teaspoon, to leave the edible base.
3 Spoon plenty of sauce into the artichoke centre. Place the artichokes on plates and eat by plucking out a leaf and dipping it into the sauce. Use your teeth to pull away the edible fleshy part at the base of the leaf, then discard the rest.

Note: Serving artichokes in this classic way is simpler than you may think. And the best bit - the base of the artichoke covered with rich, creamy sauce - is saved until last.

Serves 4
Preparation 20mins
+ 30mins cooling
Cooking 1–1½hrs
Calories 168
Fat 13g

Zucchini Rounds with Capsicum Purée

Serves 4
Preparation 15mins
+ 30mins standing
+ 1hr chilling
Cooking 20mins
Calories 168
Fat 12g

3 zucchinis, grated
salt
4 tbsp snipped fresh chives,
plus extra to garnish
2 tbsp chopped fresh coriander,
plus extra leaves to garnish
¹/₂ tsp grated nutmeg
1 spring onion, finely chopped,
to garnish

Purée
3 tbsp olive oil
3 red capsicums, cored,
deseeded and chopped
salt and black pepper

1 Sprinkle the zucchinis with salt, place in a colander, then set aside for 30 minutes to draw out the excess moisture. Rinse under cold running water, then squeeze dry and mix with the chives, coriander and nutmeg.

Pack the mixture into 4 ramekins - it should half-fill them. Refrigerate for 1 hour, or overnight.
2 To make the purée. Put the oil into a saucepan, then add the capsicums and season. Cook, covered, over a low heat for 15 minutes. Leave to cool for a few minutes, then blend to a smooth purée in a food processor, or with a hand blender. Press the purée through a sieve to remove the skins.
3 To serve, turn each ramekin onto a plate, giving it a sharp shake to dislodge the zucchini round, then spoon around the sauce. Garnish with the chives, spring onion and coriander.

Sweet Pepper Terrine with Basil Vinaigrette

butter for greasing
2 red and 2 yellow capsicums,
halved and deseeded
4 tbsp olive oil
1 red chilli, deseeded
and thinly sliced
225g/8oz tub ricotta
115g/4oz mature Cheddar, grated
1 tbsp Dijon mustard
1 tsp salt
3 medium eggs, beaten

Vinaigrette
2 tbsp white wine vinegar
2 tbsp extra virgin olive oil
5 tbsp sunflower oil
2 spring onions, finely sliced
3 tbsp finely chopped fresh basil
salt and black pepper

1 Preheat the oven to 190°C/375°F/ Gas 5. Butter a large piece of baking paper and line a 1 lb/450g loaf tin, leaving enough paper to cover the top. Finely dice ¹/₂ a red and ¹/₂ a yellow capsicum and set aside. Roughly chop the rest.

2 Heat the oil in a heavy-based saucepan, add the chopped capsicums and chilli, then cook, covered, for 20 minutes or until softened. Purée in a food processor or with a hand blender, then press through a sieve. Combine the ricotta, Cheddar, mustard, salt and eggs, then stir in the purée and diced capsicums. Pour into the tin, then fold the paper over to cover the terrine without touching. Place in a roasting tin.

3 Pour in enough boiling water to reach halfway up the sides of the loaf tin, then cook for 1 hour 15 minutes, adding more water if necessary. Cool for 2 hours, then place in the fridge for 1 hour. Invert onto a plate and peel off the paper.

4 To make the vinaigrette. Combine the ingredients, mixing well. Serve the terrine in slices with the vinaigrette.

OVEN TEMPERATURE
190°C, 375°F, GAS 5

Serves 6
Preparation 25mins
+ 2hrs cooling
1hr chilling
Cooking 1¹/₂–2hrs
Calories 439
Fat 40g

Watercress Roulade with Parmesan

OVEN TEMPERATURE
200°C, 400°F, GAS 6

Note: This is a really quick way to make a roulade. The cream cheese filling complements the peppery watercress perfectly in this deliciously light summer starter.

vegetable oil for greasing
1 tbsp freshly grated Parmesan
85g/3oz watercress, finely chopped, thick stems discarded
4 medium eggs, beaten
salt and black pepper

Filling
200g/7oz full-fat soft cheese, at room temperature
3 tbsp full-fat milk
85g/3oz watercress, finely chopped and thick stems discarded, with a few sprigs reserved to garnish
5 spring onions, finely chopped
salt and black pepper

1 Preheat the oven. Grease a 23cm x 30cm/9in x 12in swiss roll tin, line with baking paper, then sprinkle with ¹/₂ the Parmesan.
2 Mix together the watercress and eggs, season, then pour into the tin. Cook for 7–8 minutes, until the eggs have set. Remove from the oven and leave to cool for 5 minutes.
Sprinkle over the remaining Parmesan. Lay a sheet of baking paper over the top and set aside for 35 minutes or until completely cool.
3 To make the filling. Mix the soft cheese with the milk, watercress, spring onions and seasoning. Turn the cooled roulade onto a chopping board. Peel off the top sheet of paper, then spread the filling over the base. Roll up from the short end, peeling off the paper as you go. Refrigerate for 30 minutes, then serve in slices, garnished with watercress.

Serves 4
Preparation 20mins
+ 40mins cooling
+ 30mins chilling
Cooking 1–1¹/₂ hrs
Calories 266
Fat 23g

Broccoli Soufflés with Olive Purée

1 Preheat the oven. Grease four individual ramekin dishes. Cook the broccoli in a little boiling salted water for 15 minutes until tender, then drain well. Blend to a smooth purée with the cream, egg yolks and seasoning in a food processor. Transfer to a large mixing bowl.

2 Beat the egg whites until they increase in volume 6-fold and form soft peaks. Gently fold $1/3$ of the beaten whites into the broccoli purée, using a large metal spoon. Carefully fold in the remaining whites in 2 batches, mixing well.

3 Divide the mixture between the ramekin dishes and cook for 20–25 minutes, until risen and golden. Meanwhile, purée the olives, olive oil and lemon zest and juice in a food processor or with a hand blender. Serve with the soufflés.

butter for greasing
1 lb/455g broccoli, chopped
285mL/10 fl oz light cream
4 medium eggs, separated
salt and black pepper

Olive Purée
20 pitted black olives
115mL/4fl oz olive oil
grated zest and juice of 1 lemon

Serves 4
Preparation 15mins
Cooking 40mins
Calories 504
Fat 48g

OVEN TEMPERATURE
220°C, 425°F, GAS 7

Note: This method of making soufflés is easier than most. They may not rise as much, but they're unlikely to be a disaster! The olive purée gives them a rich taste. Serve with bread.

Stuffed Tomatoes with Chickpeas and Coriander

OVEN TEMPERATURE
160°C, 325°F, GAS 3

Note: A fabulous combination of chickpeas, lemon and garlic flavour, this Middle Eastern filling, is stuffed into baked tomatoes.

Serves 4
Preparation 20mins
Cooking 50mins
Calories 112
Fat 1g

2 slices day-old brown bread
4 large slicing tomatoes
1 clove garlic, crushed
100g/3¹/₂ oz canned chickpeas, drained
juice of 1 lemon
1 tbsp olive oil, plus extra for greasing
1 red onion, finely chopped
¹/₄ tsp cayenne pepper
1 tsp ground cumin
1 tsp ground coriander
4 tbsp chopped fresh coriander
salt and black pepper

1 Preheat the oven. Place the bread in the oven for 20 minutes or until it becomes crisp. Process in a food processor to make breadcrumbs. Alternatively, use a grater. Increase the oven temperature to moderately hot 200°C/400°F/Gas 6.

2 Slice off the tomato tops and scoop out the insides. Place the shells upside-down on kitchen towels to drain. Put the insides and tops into a food processor with the garlic, chickpeas and lemon juice and blend to a purée, or use a hand blender.
3 Heat the oil, then cook the onion with the cayenne pepper, cumin and ground coriander for 4–5 minutes, until softened. Mix with the tomato mixture, breadcrumbs, fresh coriander and seasoning.
4 Spoon the mixture into the tomato shells. Place them on a lightly greased baking sheet and cook for 25 minutes or until the tomatoes are tender.

Baked Onions with Mushrooms and Pine Nuts

2 slices brown bread
4 large red onions
2 tbsp olive oil
2 cloves garlic, chopped
2 tbsp pine nut kernels
200g/7oz mushrooms,
finely chopped
4 tbsp chopped fresh parsley
salt and black pepper

Serves 4
Preparation 20mins
+ 20mins cooling
Cooking 1-1½ hrs
Calories 238
Fat 14g

OVEN TEMPERATURE
160°C, 325°F, GAS 3

Note: Baked onions have a sweet, mellow flavour that goes well with this rich mushroom and herby pine nut stuffing. Serve them with bread and a leafy salad.

1 Preheat the oven. Place the bread in the oven for 20 minutes or until it becomes crisp. Process in a food processor to make breadcrumbs. Alternatively, use a grater.

2 Meanwhile, slice the tops and bases off the onions. Place in a saucepan, cover with water and bring to the boil. Cook for 10 minutes to soften. Drain, then leave to cool for 20 minutes.

3 Increase the oven to 200°C/400°F/Gas 6. Cut out the middle of each onion, leaving the shell intact, and finely chop. Heat the oil, then fry the garlic and chopped onion for 5 minutes. Add the pine nuts and mushrooms and fry for a further 5 minutes. Remove from the heat, then mix in the breadcrumbs, parsley and seasoning. Fill the onion shells with the mixture, then wrap each onion in foil, leaving the tops open. Place on a baking sheet and cook for 40 minutes or until the onions are tender.

Asparagus Polonaise

Serves 4
Preparation 40mins
Cooking 15mins
Calories 225
Fat 6g

900g/2 lb fresh asparagus
salt
3 tbsp butter
45g/1¹/₂ oz breadcrumbs, made
from stale bread
3 hard boiled egg yolks, chopped
1 tbsp chopped fresh parsley

1 First prepare the asparagus. Wash well to remove any grit and snap off the woody ends by bending each spear between your thumb and forefinger. Peel the spear ²/₃ the way up to create a beautiful contrast of pale and dark greens when cooked. Tie the asparagus into 1–2 bundles.

Place any trimmings and enough boiling salted water in a deep saucepan to fill it by ¹/₃.
2 Stand the asparagus upright in the pan, cover with a lid or dome of aluminium foil and place over a moderate heat. Bring to the boil, lower the heat and simmer for 15 minutes or until the asparagus is just tender. Drain and arrange on a heated serving plate. Keep warm.
3 Heat the butter in a small frying pan over a moderate heat and fry the breadcrumbs, stirring, until golden. Stir in the egg yolks and parsley, heat through and spoon over the asparagus. Serve immediately.

Spinach and Ricotta Bake

1 tbsp olive oil
1 onion, chopped
900g/2 lb frozen whole leaf
spinach, defrosted
255g/9oz ricotta
85g/3oz pine nut kernels
$1/4$ tsp ground nutmeg
salt and black pepper
6 sheets filo pastry
1–2 tbsp olive oil for brushing
1 beaten egg for glazing

1 Preheat the oven. Heat the oil in a heavy-based frying pan, add the onion and fry for 3–4 minutes, until slightly softened.

2 Put the spinach into a colander, press to squeeze out any excess water, then roughly chop. Place in a bowl and add the onion, ricotta, pine nuts and nutmeg. Season with salt and plenty of pepper and mix well.
3 Lightly oil a 30cm x 25cm/12in x 10in ovenproof dish. Add the spinach mixture, pressing down gently to form an even layer. Place a sheet of filo on top, folding it to fit the tin, then lightly brush with oil. Repeat with the remaining filo, brushing each sheet with oil before placing the next on top.
4 Mark the top into 6 portions using a sharp knife, then brush with the egg. Cook for 25 minutes or until golden brown.

OVEN TEMPERATURE
200°C, 400°F, GAS 4

Serves 6
Preparation 15mins
Cooking 30mins
Calories 312
Fat 22g

Note: This Greek-style bake is a real classic and always goes down well. Add a good helping of mature Cheddar or another hard cheese to the filling for extra punch.

Salads

Feeling tired, jaded or run down? Sounds like you haven't had your vegetable therapy. 'Three veg' just doesn't cut it these days; what you need is a high-yield salad infusion. Tofu, lentils, Bulgur wheat, asparagus, celery, avocado, snow peas and four types of mushrooms. They're all waiting to make you feel like a million bucks. Whether you toss, dress or warm them, these exotic and familiar creations will take care of you like only Mother Nature knows how.

Warm Spinach Salad with Walnuts

*Note: There's
something seductive
about warm salads -
their flavours seem
more intense. In this
easy salad, walnuts,
spinach and sun-
dried tomatoes create
a magical result.*

2 tbsp walnut oil
5 sun-dried tomatoes in oil,
drained and chopped
225g/8oz baby spinach
1 red onion, sliced into thin rings
2 tbsp walnut pieces
salt
3 tbsp chopped fresh coriander
to garnish

1 Heat the oil in a wok or large,
heavy-based frying pan. Add the
tomatoes, spinach, onion, walnut
pieces and salt to taste. Cook for 1
minute or until the spinach begins
to wilt, tossing to combine.
2 Transfer the vegetables to a large
salad bowl and sprinkle with the
coriander to garnish.
Serve immediately away.

Photograph appears also on page 24

Serves 4
Preparation 5mins
Cooking 5mins
Calories 166
Fat 15g

Italian Eggplant Salad

1 large eggplant
¹/₄ cup vegetable oil
2 cloves garlic
¹/₄ cup red wine vinegar
¹/₃ cup olive oil
¹/₃ cup chopped parsley
snipped basil leaves or dill to
salt and black pepper
1 red capsicum
1 salad onion, finely chopped

1 Cut the eggplant into cubes and fry very gently in a covered pan until pale golden and tender. Allow to cool in a colander to help drain the excess oil.

2 Meanwhile, use a food processor, puree the garlic with the vinegar, olive oil, parsley, basil or dill and salt and pepper to taste.

3 Toss the eggplant in the dressing in a salad bowl. Char the capsicum over a gas flame or under a hot griller until the skin is blackened all over. Now scrape away the blackened skin, rinsing frequently in cold water. When all the pepper is peeled, halve it, flick out the seeds and cut the pepper in large chunks. If you prefer, canned pepper (pimientos) can be used instead. Add to the salad and scatter with the onion.

Serves 4
Preparation 20mins
Cooking nil
Calories 339
Fat 3g

Mushroom and Snow Pea Salad

Serves 4
Preparation 5mins
Cooking 1min
Calories 291
Fat 24g

225g/8oz fresh mushrooms
115g/4oz snow peas
$^1/_2$ cup mayonnaise
1 tbsp lime or lemon juice
4 tbsp light sour cream
1 tbsp each chopped parsley,
chervil and snipped chives
salt and freshly ground pepper

1 Slice the mushrooms very finely. String the snow peas, drop into boiling water for about 10 seconds, drain and refresh in cold water. Cut each one into 3 diagonal pieces. Place in a bowl with the mushrooms.
2 In another bowl combine the mayonnaise with the sour cream, herbs and salt and pepper.
3 Fold the dressing into the mushrooms. Turn into a serving bowl and garnish with the chives.

Asparagus and Tomato Salad with Cucumber

1 large bunch asparagus
4 small ripe tomatoes
a selection of salad greens

Dressing
1 small cucumber
1 tiny spring onion
salt
freshly ground pepper
2 tbsp lemon juice
1 tbsp sour cream
3 tbsp each salad oil and hazelnut
or virgin olive oil
2 tbsp chopped dill

1 First prepare the dressing. Peel the cucumber lightly and remove the seeds.

Cut the cucumber into chunks, roughly chop the spring onion and sprinkle them both with salt. Leave to drain for 1 hour in a colander. Rinse in cold water and drain again thoroughly. Puree in a blender or food processor, add the salt, pepper, lemon juice, sour cream and oils (last), until a smooth dressing is formed. Add the dill and chill.

2 Prepare and cook the asparagus and cut into 4cm/1¹/₂in pieces. Peel the tomatoes, halve them and remove the seeds. Cut each half into strips.

3 Arrange the salad greens on serving plates.

4 Toss the asparagus and tomato in the dressing and arrange on each plate.

Serves 4
Preparation 10mins
Cooking 10min
Calories 335
Fat 14g

American Potato Salad

Idea: To serve new potatoes-remove the skin, wash and boil in salted water. Drain and add chopped spring onions some butter and a heaped teaspoon of rolled oats. Toss all together in a pan and cook through.

Serves 4
Preparation 20min
Cooking 20min
Calories 257
Fat 1g

900g/2 lb new potatoes
salted water
$^1/_3$ cup dry white wine
$^1/_2$ cup vinaigrette dressing
1 red onion, sliced into rings
1 stalk celery, sliced
2 dill pickles or gherkins,
thinly sliced
1 tsp capers
4 hard boiled eggs,
peeled and sliced
chopped parsley
salt and freshly ground pepper

1 Scrub and boil the potatoes in salted water until tender . Peel and slice them while still hot into a bowl. Sprinkle with wine, turning the potato slices carefully. Now sprinkle with the vinaigrette dressing and add the remaining ingredients. Season with salt and pepper to serve.

Variation with mayonnaise:
Follow the recipe and fold in $^1/_2$ cup of mayonnaise or $^1/_4$ cup each sour cream and mayonnaise before adding the remaining ingredients. This is easy to do because the potatoes are already oil coated, which also means less mayonnaise is needed.

Lettuce, Avocado and Peanut Salad

2 crispy lettuces, leaves separated
1 head Belgium endive,
leaves separated
2 small ripe avocados, stoned,
peeled and cut into chunks
3 spring onions, chopped
3 tbsp salted peanuts

Dressing
1 tbsp lemon juice
1 clove garlic, crushed
3 tbsp olive oil
2 tbsp smooth peanut butter
salt and black pepper

1 To make the dressing. Put the lemon juice, garlic, oil and peanut butter into a bowl, combine thoroughly and season.

2 Arrange the lettuce leaves, endive and avocado in a large shallow dish. Pour over the dressing and sprinkle with spring onions and peanuts.

Note: Nutty tastes and textures work well with the avocados and bitter-leafed endive in this salad. Serve as a starter with some chilled Chardonnay.

Serves 4
Preparation 15mins
Calories 332
Fat 32g

Celery, Carrot and Apple Salad with Tahini

Note: A dash of lemon juice adds sharpness to thick tahini paste, made from sesame seeds. With a little crushed garlic, it makes a great dressing for this colourful salad.

3 carrots, grated
1 celery heart, thinly sliced
2 eating apples, peeled, cored and thinly sliced

Dressing
3 tbsp lemon juice
1 clove garlic, crushed
2 tbsp tahini paste
salt

1 To make the dressing. Place the lemon juice, garlic, tahini paste and 3 tablespoons of water in a food processor and blend until smooth. Alternatively, combine with a fork. Season to taste.
2 Toss together the carrots, celery heart and apples and transfer to individual serving bowls. Drizzle over the dressing.

Serves 4
Preparation 15mins
Calories 99
Fat 4g

Pasta and Asparagus Salad

500g/1 lb chilli linguine
225g/8oz asparagus, cut in half
145g/5oz watercress, broken into
sprigs
55g/2oz butter
2 tbsp chopped
fresh rosemary
freshly ground black pepper
fresh Parmesan cheese shavings
lime wedges

Serves 4
Preparation 10mins
Cooking 25mins
Calories 538
Fat 7.6g

*Note: Chilli pasta
is available from
delicatessens and
specialty food stores.
If unavailable use
ordinary pasta and
add some chopped
fresh chilli to the
butter and rosemary
mixture.*

1 Cook pasta in boiling water in a
large saucepan following packet
directions. Drain, rinse under cold
running water, drain again and set
aside.
2 Boil, steam or microwave
asparagus until tender. Add
asparagus and watercress to pasta
and toss to combine.
3 Place butter and rosemary in a
small saucepan and cook over a low
heat until butter is golden. Divide
pasta between serving bowls, then
drizzle with rosemary-flavoured
butter and top with black pepper
and Parmesan cheese to taste.
Serve with lime wedges.

Spicy Wild Rice Salad

Serves 4
Preparation 15mins
Cooking 25mins
Calories 1045
Fat 6.6g

Note: If wild rice blend is unavailable use ³/₄ cup brown rice and ¹/₄ cup wild rice. The two varieties of rice can be cooked together.

400g/14oz wild rice blend
(brown and wild rice mix)
2 tbsp vegetable oil
2 onions, cut into thin wedges
1 tsp ground cumin
¹/₂ tsp ground cinnamon
¹/₄ tsp ground cloves
¹/₄ tsp ground ginger
2 carrots, thinly sliced
1 tsp honey
2 oranges, segmented
85g/3oz pistachios, toasted
and roughly chopped
85g/3oz raisins
55g/2oz flaked almonds, toasted
3 spring onions, sliced
3 tbsp chopped fresh dill

Dressing
1 tsp Dijon mustard
¹/₂ cup olive oil
¹/₄ cup orange juice
1 tbsp red wine vinegar

1 Cook rice in boiling water following packet directions or until tender. Drain well and set aside to cool.
2 Heat oil in a nonstick frying pan over a medium heat, add onions, cumin, cinnamon, cloves and ginger and cook, stirring, for 10 minutes or until onions are soft and slightly caramelised. Add carrots and cook until tender. Stir in honey, then remove from heat and cool slightly.
3 Place rice, carrot mixture, oranges, pistachios, raisins, almonds, spring onions and dill in a bowl and toss to combine.
4 To make dressing, place mustard, oil, orange juice and vinegar in a bowl and whisk to combine.
Pour dressing over salad and toss.

Oriental Coleslaw

1 daikon (white radish)
1 large carrot
$^1/_2$ Chinese cabbage, shredded
$^1/_4$ red cabbage, shredded
2 green onions,
cut into long thin strips
18 snow peas, cut lengthwise into
thin strips
1 cup shredded spinach
$^1/_2$ cup raisins
$^1/_2$ cup slivered unsalted almonds,
toasted (optional)

Dressing
2 tbsp sesame seeds
3 tsp grated fresh ginger or
shredded pickled ginger
1 tsp sugar
3 tbsp rice wine (mirin) or sherry
2 tbsp rice
or wine vinegar
2 tsp macadamia or peanut oil
2 tsp reduced-salt soy sauce
few drops sesame oil (optional)

1 Using a zester, Japanese grater or sharp knife, cut the daikon and carrot into long thin strips. Place in a large bowl. Add the Chinese and red cabbages, green onions, snow peas, spinach, raisins and almonds. Toss to combine.

2 To make the dressing. Place the sesame seeds in a small saucepan over a medium heat. Cook, shaking the pan frequently, for 2–3 minutes or until the seeds are toasted. Stir in the ginger, sugar, mirin or sherry, vinegar, macadamia or peanut oil, soy sauce and sesame oil (if using). Remove the pan from the heat. Immediately pour over the salad. Toss to combine.

Serves 6
Preparation 10mins
Calories 178
Fat 12g

Bulgar Wheat Salad with Grilled Peppers

Note: This salad is delicious, filling and extremely nutritious. The mustard and balsamic vinegar in the dressing bring all the other exciting flavours alive.

Serves 4
Preparation 35mins
(including soaking time)
Cooking 20min
Calories 480
Fat 26g

225g/8oz bulgur wheat
2 yellow capsicums, quartered and deseeded
255g/9oz green beans, halved
2 ripe tomatoes
4 spring onions, sliced
85g/3oz brazil nuts, roughly chopped
4 tbsp chopped fresh parsley
sea salt and freshly ground black pepper

Dressing
4 tbsp extra virgin olive oil
1 tbsp wholegrain mustard
1 garlic clove, crushed
1 tsp balsamic vinegar
1 tsp white wine vinegar

1 Place the bulgur in a bowl and pour over boiling water to about 2cm/$^3/_4$ in above the level of the bulgur and leave to soak for 20 minutes. Meanwhile, preheat the grill to high. Grill the capsicums, skin-side up, for 15–20 minutes, until the skin is blistered and blackened all over. Transfer to a plastic bag, seal and leave to cool. When cold enough to handle, remove and discard the charred skins and roughly chop the flesh.
2 Blanch the beans in boiling water for 3–4 minutes, drain, refresh under cold running water and set aside. Put the tomatoes into a bowl, cover with boiling water and leave for 30 seconds. Peel, deseed, then roughly chop the flesh.
3 Combine the ingredients for the dressing and mix well. Drain the bulgur and transfer to a salad bowl. Add the dressing and toss well. Add the vegetables, spring onions, brazil nuts, parsley and seasoning and toss together gently to mix.

Grilled Brie with Beet Salad

1 avocado
225g/8oz cooked beets, drained
and chopped
2 celery sticks, sliced
1 red dessert apple, cored
and chopped
4 slices stonebaked white loaf
1 portion Dutch Brie, approx.
115g/4oz quartered
115g/4oz Alfresco salad

Dressing
3 tbsp extra virgin olive oil
3 tbsp cider vinegar
1 garlic clove, crushed
1 small red onion,
finely chopped
1 tbsp tomato purée
sea salt and freshly ground
black pepper

1 Peel and slice the avocado and place in a bowl together with the beet, celery and apple. Cover and set aside. Preheat the grill to high and lightly toast the bread for 2–3 minutes each side. Place a slice of Brie on top of each toast, then return them to the grill. Cook until the cheese is melted and slightly golden.
2 Meanwhile, make the dressing. Place all the ingredients in a small saucepan and bring to the boil. Simmer for 2–3 minutes, until warmed through.
3 To serve, divide the salad leaves between 4 plates, top with the beet mixture and place a cheese toast on each plate. Drizzle over the warm dressing and serve immediately.

Note: Creamy Brie, crusty bread, crisp apples and celery and sweet, soft beet make a wonderful contrast of flavours and textures.

Serves 4
Preparation 15mins
Cooking 6–10mins
Calories 403
Fat 25g

Zucchini and Hazelnut Salad

Note: This salad combines all sorts of flavours and textures: pan-fried zucchinis, crumbled feta and toasted hazelnuts. It tastes amazing and is really quick to make.

Serves 6
Preparation 15mins
Cooking 2–5mins
Calories 315
Fat 29g

680g/1½ lb small zucchinis
2 tbsp sunflower oil, plus extra for frying
5 tbsp walnut oil
1 tbsp white wine vinegar
salt and black pepper
115g/4oz whole blanched hazelnuts
170g/6oz watercress, thick stalks removed
85g/3oz feta, crumbled

1 Pare the zucchinis lengthways into slivers using a vegetable peeler. In a bowl, mix together the oils, and vinegar and season. Add ¹/₂ the zucchini slivers to the mixture, toss lightly and set aside.
2 Brush a large frying pan with a little sunflower oil and heat.

Lay the remaining zucchini slivers in the pan and cook for 2 minutes on each side or until lightly charred. Remove, season and set aside. Wipe the pan clean.
3 Roughly crush the hazelnuts, using a mortar and pestle, or put them in a plastic bag, seal and crush with a rolling pin. Place in the frying pan and fry for 1–2 minutes, until golden.
4 Divide the watercress between serving plates. Spoon some of the marinated zucchinis into the centre, reserving some of the marinade. Scatter over ½ the toasted hazelnuts and the feta. Arrange the charred zucchinis on top, sprinkle over the rest of the hazelnuts and the reserved marinade.

Vietnamese Herbed Rice Noodles with Peanuts and Asparagus

3 tbsp rice vinegar
1 tbsp sugar
1 small Spanish onion,
finely sliced
225g/8oz dried rice noodles
2 bunches asparagus
⅓ cup chopped fresh mint
⅓ cup chopped fresh coriander
1 continental cucumber, peeled,
seeded and thinly sliced
6 spring onions, finely sliced
3 plum tomatoes, finely diced
¾ cup roasted peanuts, lightly
crushed
juice of 2 limes
2 tsp fish sauce
2 tsp olive oil
½ tsp chilli flakes

1 First, whisk the vinegar and sugar together and pour over the onion rings. Allow to marinate for 1 hour, tossing frequently.
2 Cook the noodles according to packet directions (usually, rice noodles need only soak in boiling water for 5 minutes; otherwise, boil for 1–2 minutes then drain immediately and rinse under cold water).
3 Cut the tough stalks off the asparagus, and cut the remaining stalks into 2cm/³/₄in lengths. Simmer the asparagus in salted water for 2 minutes until bright green and crisp-tender. Rinse in cold water to refresh.

4 Toss the noodles with the reserved onion/vinegar mixture while still warm, then using kitchen scissors, cut the noodles into manageable lengths.
5 To the noodles, add the cooked asparagus, mint, coriander, cucumber, spring onions, tomatoes and peanuts and toss thoroughly.
6 Whisk the lime juice, fish sauce, oil and chilli flakes together and drizzle over the noodle salad. Serve at room temperature.

Serves 4
Preparation 10mins
Cooking 10mins
Calories 335
Fat 14g

Main Courses

At last you can learn to create gnocchi. Finally you can find out why people stuff eggplants. And now you can make the most of that strange material they call 'filo'. The common thread, of course, is vegetables. But how different and exciting they look when you know what to do with them! Get set for a journey of discovery, where things are not all they seem. Strudel without apple, lasagna without meat and butter beans without a peep of protest. These wonders and more await your enjoyment.

Roasted Vegetable and Broccoli Couscous

OVEN TEMPERATURE
200°C, 400°F, GAS 6

Note: When they're roasted, vegetables caramelise naturally. Glazing them with apple or redcurrant jelly adds extra gloss and makes them taste even sweeter.

**4 parsnips, cut into chunks
2 sweet potatoes, cut into chunks
4 turnips, quartered
2 cloves garlic, crushed
6 tbsp olive oil
salt
5 tbsp apple or redcurrant jelly
285g/10oz couscous
500g/1 lb tomatoes, chopped
handful each of chopped fresh parsley, chives and basil
juice of 1 lemon
285g/10oz broccoli, cut into florets**

Photograph appears also on page 40

1 Preheat the oven. Cook the parsnips in a saucepan of boiling salted water for 2 minutes, then drain. Place in a roasting tin with the sweet potatoes, turnips, garlic and 3 tablespoons of oil, turning to coat. Sprinkle with salt, then cook for 30 minutes or until lightly browned.

2 Melt the apple or redcurrant jelly in a pan with 4 tablespoons of water for 2–3 minutes, until it turns syrupy. Turn the vegetables in the tin and carefully spoon over the syrup. Return to the oven for 10 minutes or until browned and glossy.

3 Meanwhile, prepare the couscous according to the packet instructions. Heat the rest of the oil in a frying pan and cook the tomatoes for 2–3 minutes, until softened. Add the couscous and heat through, then mix in the herbs and lemon juice. Meanwhile, boil the broccoli florets for 2 minutes or until tender, then drain. Serve the couscous with the roasted vegetables and broccoli arranged on top.

Serves 4
Preparation 20mins
Cooking 50mins
Calories 442
Fat 20g

Fusilli with Eggplant and Tomatoes

2 medium eggplant
$^1/_2$ cup olive oil
1 clove garlic
4 medium tomatoes
salt and pepper
1–2 tbsp chopped basil
2 tbsp grated Parmesan
300g/10$^1/_2$oz fusilli (spirals)
freshly ground black pepper

1 Peel eggplant and cut into small dice.
2 Pour $^1/_2$ the oil into a frying pan and add the garlic and diced eggplant. Fry gently until tender.
3 Meanwhile, skin the tomatoes, remove the seeds and dice the flesh.
4 Pour the remaining oil into the frying pan and add the diced tomatoes. Cook for about 5 minutes and add salt, pepper and basil.
5 Meanwhile cook the fusilli in boiling, salted water for 10–12 minutes until 'al dente'. Drain. Toss in the eggplant and tomatoes and sprinkle with Parmesan and black pepper, mixing well.

Serves 4
Preparation 20mins
Cooking 15mins
Calories 576
Fat 4g

Potato Gnocchi

Serves 4
Preparation 5mins
Cooking 10-15mins
Calories 291
Fat 24g

900g/2 lb old floury potatoes
1³/₄ cups plain flour
salt

1 Scrub the potatoes and place in a pan with just enough water to cover them. Cover and boil the potatoes until tender without letting them break up. Drain and peel them as soon as you can handle them. Mash and rub them through a metal sieve using the base of a glass or jar to help.
2 As soon as the puree is cool enough to handle, start beating in the flour, then as the dough stiffens, turn it out to knead on a floured board. Knead until you have a soft and elastic dough.
3 Next, take a handful of the dough and knead lightly, using flour to dust your hands and the work surface. Roll the dough into a sausage shape. Cut into 2cm/¹/₂ in slices.
4 Take a large, slim pronged fork with round edges. A wooden fork is best but difficult to find. Hold it in your left hand with the prongs down. Take a slice of dough and gently press the dough against the prongs with your thumb, letting the gnocchi roll off on to a clean cloth. Repeat with remaining dough. The gnocchi should curl up into crescent-shaped, ribbed shells as they roll off the fork. A simpler alternative, if you're finding this shaping difficult to master, is to press each slice of dough gently around your finger to curve it, using a fork to make the ribbed grooves.

The shaping is not just decorative. It serves to thin out the centre of the gnocchi so they cook evenly, and the grooves serve to trap the of the sauce.
5 Drop the gnocchi (about 20 at a time) into a large pan of boiling salted water. When they're ready they will float to the surface. Cook them for just another 10 seconds, then remove with a slotted spoon to a warm dish. Sprinkle them with freshly grated parmesan cheese and pieces of butter and toss lightly. Serve immediately.

Gnocchi with Tomato and Basil Sauce

1–1¹/₂ lb/455g–680g ripe red tomatoes
3 tbs olive oil
10 basil leaves
salt and freshly ground black pepper
¹/₂ cup freshly grated Parmesan

1 Peel the tomatoes and chop them roughly. Add to a pan in which the oil has been heated, with any juice from the tomatoes. Simmer for 10–15 minutes, stirring from time to time until the sauce has begun to thicken. Add the basil, salt and pepper.
2 Cook the gnocchi as described, drain and toss with the sauce and Parmesan.
3 Serve immediately.

Roman Stuffed Tomatoes

OVEN TEMPERATURE
190°C, 375°F, GAS 5

Serves 6
Preparation 15mins
Cooking 15mins
Calories 285
Fat 1¹/₂g

6 large tomatoes
1¹/₂ cups cooked long grain rice
(²/₃ cup uncooked)
2 tbsp chopped fresh basil
¹/₄ cup olive oil
4 canned anchovy fillets, drained
and chopped
2 cloves garlic, crushed
sugar
freshly ground black pepper

1 Slice the caps off the tomatoes and set aside. Use a teaspoon to scoop some of the flesh out of each tomato, leaving a thick shell. Roughly chop the inside tomato flesh and mix it with the remaining ingredients, seasoning with salt and pepper.
2 Stand the tomatoes in an oiled shallow ovenproof dish just large enough to hold them in one layer and fill them with the rice mixture. Top with the caps.
3 Bake in a moderately hot oven for 15 minutes, basting with cooking juices every now and then.
4 Serve hot or at room temperature.

Italian Spinach Tart

Pastry
2 cups flour
pinch salt
115g/4oz sweet butter
¹/₃ cup iced water

Filling
455g/1 lb spinach
200g/7oz fresh ricotta
4 eggs, beaten
55g/2oz grated Parmesan
grated nutmeg
salt and freshly ground
black pepper

1 Sift the flour and salt into a large bowl. Cut the butter into small pieces, adding it to the flour. Rub the butter into the flour with your fingertips until the mixture resembles breadcrumbs. Don't overdo this as the butter will be blended more thoroughly later.

2 Make a well in the centre. Mix in the iced water and combine quickly with a knife. Press the dough together with your fingers.

3 Turn out on to a floured board and knead lightly until smooth. Roll into a ball. Brush off excess flour. Wrap in waxed paper and chill for 20–30 minutes before using.

4 Roll out the pastry and use it to line a 25cm/10in flan ring. Trim the edges. Prick the base lightly with a fork and line with baking paper. Half fill with dried beans and bake 'blind' in a preheated hot oven for 7 minutes. Remove the beans and bake for a further 5 minutes.

5 Meanwhile, wash and cook the spinach with just the water clinging to the leaves, in a covered pan. When tender, drain, squeeze dry, cool and chop finely. In a bowl, beat the ricotta until smooth, then beat in the eggs, Parmesan and spinach. Season the mixture and pour it into the pre-baked pastry shell. Reduce oven temperature and bake in a moderate oven 180°C/350°F/Gas 4 for 25–30 minutes until golden and set.

OVEN TEMPERATURE
200°F, 400°C, GAS 6

Serves 4
Preparation 20mins
Cooking 1hr
Calories 693
Fat 23g

Baked Eggplants with Gruyere

OVEN TEMPERATURE
200°C, 400°F, GAS 6

Serves 4
Preparation 15mins
Cooking 15–20mins
Calories 242
Fat 18g

Note: Eggplants are one of the best vegetables for stuffing. The shells hold their shape well and there's just enough room for the filling. A salad and crusty bread complete the meal.

2 tbsp olive oil, plus extra
for greasing and brushing
2 eggplants
455g/1 lb tomatoes, chopped
1 tbsp dried oregano
3 cloves garlic, chopped
salt and black pepper
2 tbsp tomato paste
115g/4oz Gruyère, thinly sliced

1 Preheat the oven. Lightly grease a baking sheet. Slice the eggplants down the middle lengthways. Use a knife and spoon to gouge out the flesh, taking care not to pierce the skin. Chop the flesh into chunks.
2 Place the eggplant flesh in a saucepan with the tomatoes, oregano, garlic, oil and seasoning. Cook gently, uncovered, for 5 minutes or until slightly softened, stirring occasionally. Add the tomato paste and cook for 5 minutes or until the mixture has thickened and reduced.
3 Meanwhile, place the eggplant halves on the baking sheet, brush the insides with oil and cook for 10–12 minutes, until almost tender. Fill the eggplants with the tomato mixture, cover with the Gruyère and return to the oven. Cook for 10 minutes or until the cheese has browned.

Mushroom and Black Olive Risotto

30g/1oz dried
porcini mushrooms
3 tbsp olive oil
1 onion, chopped
225g/8oz large open mushrooms,
chopped
255g/9oz risotto rice (arborio)
2 cups vegetable stock
2 tbsp black olives, pitted and
roughly chopped
salt and black pepper
2 tbsp black olive paste
fresh Parmesan to serv

1 Cover the porcini with 200mL/7fl oz of boiling water, then leave to soak for 20 minutes. Drain, reserving the water, and set aside. Heat the oil in a large heavy-based saucepan, add the onion and fresh mushrooms and fry for 4–5 minutes. Add the rice and stir to coat with the oil. Fry for 1–2 minutes.

2 Add the porcini and the reserved liquid to the rice with 1 cup of the vegetable stock and the olives. Simmer, covered, for 10 minutes or until the liquid has been absorbed, stirring occasionally.

3 Stir in $\frac{1}{2}$ of the remaining stock and cook for 5 minutes, covered, until absorbed. Add the rest of the stock, the seasoning and the olive paste and cook for 5 minutes, uncovered, stirring constantly. Remove from the heat and leave to rest, covered, for 5 minutes.

Shave over the Parmesan, using a vegetable peeler, then serve.

Serves 4
Preparation
10mins plus
20mins
soaking and
5mins resting
Cooking 15–20mins
Calories 431
Fat 19g

Tortilla with Corn and Sun-Dried Tomatoes

225g/8oz potatoes, thickly sliced
3 tbsp olive oil
3 tbsp canned corn, drained
4 sun-dried tomatoes in oil,
drained and chopped
2 tbsp chopped fresh parsley
6 medium eggs, beaten
salt and black pepper

Note: You can choose any combination of vegetables and herbs you like for this Spanish-style omelette, but make quite sure the potato is crisp and golden before pouring in the egg.

Serves 4
Preparation 15mins
Cooking 20–25mins
Calories 324
Fat 23g

1 Boil the potatoes for 10 minutes and leave to cool slightly. Heat the oil in a large, flameproof, heavy-based frying pan, add the potatoes and fry over a high heat for 2–3 minutes, until browned and crisp. Reduce the heat, then stir in the corn and tomatoes and heat through for 1–2 minutes.
2 Preheat the grill to medium. Add the parsley to the eggs and season, then pour over the vegetables in the frying pan. Cook over a low heat for 3–4 minutes, until the omelette base is set and lightly browned.
3 Place the pan under the grill for 1–2 minutes, until the top is set and golden. Leave to cool slightly, then cut into 4 wedges and serve with salad.

Spinach and Roquefort Tart

OVEN TEMPERATURE
200°C, 400°F, GAS 6

Note: Blue cheese and cream make this spinach tart rich but irresistible. Make sure any excess water is squeezed out of the spinach for a good firm texture.

Serves 6
Preparation 20mins
+ 10mins standing
Cooking 1hr
Calories 480
Fat 37g

340g/12oz unsweetened pastry, thawed if frozen
225g/8oz fresh spinach, thick stalks discarded
black pepper
pinch of freshly grated nutmeg
115g/4oz Roquefort or other blue cheese, cubed
1 medium egg, beaten
285mL/10fl oz carton light cream

1 Preheat the oven. Roll out the pastry on a lightly floured surface and use it to line a 23cm/9in flan dish. Prick the pastry base with a fork and bake for 10 minutes or until lightly golden.

2 Meanwhile, rinse the spinach and place it in a saucepan with the water clinging to its leaves. Cook, covered, for 3–4 minutes, until wilted. Drain, leave to cool slightly, then squeeze out the excess water. Spoon the spinach into the pastry base and spread with the back of a wooden spoon. Season with pepper and nutmeg, then add the cheese. Mix together the egg and cream and pour over the top.

3 Bake for 30 minutes or until the filling has risen and is golden. Leave to rest for 10 minutes before serving in slices.

Butter Bean Tart with Caramelised Onions

225g/8oz puff pastry, defrosted if frozen
butter for greasing
2 tbsp olive oil
3 onions, sliced
salt and black pepper
1 tsp caster sugar
400g/14oz can butter beans, drained
2 tbsp freshly grated Parmesan
2 tbsp freshly grated Gruyère
3 medium eggs, beaten
5 spring onions, finely chopped
115g/4oz crème fraîche

Serves 6
Preparation 30mins
+ 10mins chilling
+ 10mins cooling
Cooking 1hr
Calories 463
Fat 31g

OVEN TEMPERATURE
220°C, 425°F, GAS 7

Note: Even people who don't like butter beans will be asking for seconds of this tart. It's the topping of crème fraîche and caramelised onions that's to blame!

1 Preheat the oven. Roll out the pastry on a lightly floured surface and use it to line a greased 20cm x 5cm/8in x 2in deep tart tin. Refrigerate for 10 minutes.

2 Heat the oil in a heavy-based saucepan, add the onions, salt and sugar and cook over a low heat for 20 minutes or until the onions have caramelised and turned golden. Set aside.

3 Purée the butter beans in a food processor or with a hand blender, or mash with a fork. Transfer to a bowl and stir in the Parmesan, Gruyère, seasoning and eggs. Mix thoroughly, then pour into the pastry case. Bake for 30–35 minutes, until the top has risen and is golden. Leave to cool for 10 minutes. Meanwhile, mix together the spring onions and crème fraîche. Spoon over the tart and top with the caramelised onions.

Tuscan Vegetable Terrine

OVEN TEMPERATURE
180°C, 350°F, GAS 4

Serves 8
Preparation 50mins
Cooking 30mins plus
refrigeration time
Calories 321
Fat 14g

300g/10¹/₂oz pumpkin, peeled
16 plum tomatoes
400g/14oz bocconcini cheese,
well-drained
1 bunch fresh basil
freshly ground black pepper

Mustard and Balsamic Dressing
1 tsp wholegrain mustard
2 tbsp balsamic vinegar
2 tbsp olive oil
1 bunch rocket
Italian bread

1 Preheat oven. Line a terrine or loaf dish with plastic food wrap, leaving enough wrap overhanging the sides to cover top of terrine. Set aside.
2 To make terrine: Cut pumpkin into 1cm/¹/₂in thick slices to fit shape of terrine–there should be enough for a single layer in the terrine. Lightly spray or brush slices with olive oil. Place on a baking tray. Bake for 20-30 minutes or until pumpkin is cooked, but still firm. Cool.
3 Cut tomatoes in half lengthwise. Remove seeds and press gently with hands to flatten. Cut cheese into 5mm/¹/₄in thick slices.
4 Layer the ingredients in the terrine in the following order – tomatoes, basil leaves, cheese, tomatoes, basil leaves, cheese, pumpkin, basil leaves, tomatoes, cheese, basil leaves, tomatoes and finally cheese. The overall effect should be layers of tomatoes, basil and cheese with a layer of pumpkin in the centre. When layering, place the tomatoes skin side down and season each tomato layer with a little black pepper. Cover terrine with the overhanging plastic wrap. Weigh down. Refrigerate overnight.
5 Dressing: Place mustard, vinegar and oil in a screwtop jar. Shake well to combine. Set aside until ready to use.
6 To serve, using the plastic wrap, carefully lift terrine from dish. Cut into thick slices. Line serving plates with rocket leaves. Place a slice of terrine on top. Drizzle with dressing. Accompany with Italian bread.

Vegetable Cannelloni

12 instant (no precooking required) cannelloni tubes
225g/8oz mozzarella cheese, grated

Leek and spinach filling
2 tsp olive oil
1 clove garlic, crushed
2 spring onions, finely chopped
2 leeks, thinly sliced
1 red capsicum, sliced
1 bunch English spinach, chopped
200g/7oz ricotta cheese, drained
315g/11oz canned creamed corn
2 tsp ground paprika

Tomato sauce
1 tsp olive oil
1 onion, chopped
400g/14oz canned tomato purée
2 tbsp dry white wine

1 To make filling, heat oil in a frying pan over a medium heat. Add garlic, spring onions and leeks and cook, stirring, for 4 minutes or until leeks are soft.
2 Add red capsicum and spinach and cook, stirring, for 3 minutes or until spinach wilts. Drain off liquid.

3 Transfer vegetable mixture to a large bowl, add ricotta cheese, corn and paprika and mix well to combine.
4 Spoon filling into cannelloni tubes and place tubes side-by-side in a greased large ovenproof dish. Set aside.
5 To make sauce, heat oil in a saucepan over a medium heat. Add onion and cook, stirring, for 3 minutes or until onion is soft. Stir in tomato purée and wine, bring to simmering and simmer for 4 minutes. Pour sauce over cannelloni tubes, sprinkle with mozzarella cheese and bake for 40 minutes or until pasta is tender and cheese is golden.

Serves 4
Preparation 25mins
Cooking 1hr
Calories 772
Fat 8.8g

Mixed Mushroom and Goat's Cheese Strudel

OVEN TEMPERATURE
180°C, 350°F, GAS 4

Makes 2 strudels -
each cuts into
4 thick slices
Preparation 25mins
Cooking 30–35mins
Calories 291
Fat 3g

1 tsp extra virgin olive oil
2 green onions, finely diced
2 cloves garlic, crushed
455g/1 lb mixed mushrooms of
your choice (e.g. shiitake, Swiss
or oyster), diced
$1/2$ cup white wine
1 tsp lemon juice
85g/3oz reduced-fat and salt
feta cheese, crumbled
3 tbsp chopped fresh mixed herbs
(e.g. sage, thyme,oregano,
rosemary)
8 sheets filo pastry
freshly ground black pepper

Dried Mushroom and Herb Broth
(optional)
2 cups water
1 cup dried mushrooms
2 tbsp no-added-salt tomato paste
1 tbsp chopped fresh herbs (e.g.
parsley, basil, chivesor coriander)
1 tbsp sherry

1 Heat the oil in a frying pan over a low heat. Add the onions and garlic. Cook, stirring, for 2–3 minutes or until soft and translucent.
Add the mushrooms. Cook, stirring occasionally, for 5–8 minutes or until juices evaporate. Stir in the wine and lemon juice. Cook, stirring occasionally, until liquid is absorbed. Cool.

2 Preheat the oven. Lightly spray or brush a baking tray with olive oil or line with nonstick baking paper. Set aside.
3 Stir the cheese and fresh herbs into mushroom mixture. Lay 2 sheets of filo pastry on a clean, dry work surface. Lightly spray or brush with olive oil and season with pepper. Place 2 more sheets on top. Place $1/2$ the mushroom mixture along the long edge leaving a 3cm/$1^1/4$ in border at each end. Fold in the ends. Roll up tightly. Place strudel seam down on prepared baking tray. Repeat with remaining filo and mushroom mixture to make a second strudel. Using a sharp knife, make slashes in the top of each strudel to mark slices. Bake for 10–12 minutes or until golden.
4 To make the broth. Place the water in a saucepan. Bring to the boil. Add mushrooms, tomato paste, herbs and sherry. Boil until the mushrooms are tender and the mixture starts to thicken.
5 Cut the strudels where marked. Serve with or without broth.

Mushroom Lasagne

Oven temperature
200°C, 400°F, Gas 6

Note: If using dried lasagne sheets, partially cook them beforehand in a large saucepan of boiling salted water to which 1 tablespoon of oil has been added for 3–5 minutes or until pliable. Drain and cool slightly.

3 tbsp olive oil
2 cloves garlic, crushed
900g/2 lb white mushrooms, finely sliced
5–6 tbsp chopped fresh parsley
1 tsp chopped fresh oregano or
$^1/_4$ tsp dried
salt and black pepper
225g/8oz fresh pasta, cut into flat sheets, or 6–8 lasagne sheets
155g/5$^1/_2$oz freshly grated Parmesan cheese

Bechamel Sauce
55g/2oz sweet butter
1 small onion, finely chopped
4 tbsp flour
4 cups hot milk
salt
freshly ground black pepper
1 large egg yolk

1 To make the sauce. Melt butter in a large saucepan over a moderate heat and cook the onion, stirring, for 5 minutes or until soft. Stir in the flour and cook for 1 minute. Remove the pan from the heat and gradually blend in the milk. Cook, stirring constantly, until the sauce boils and thickens. Season with salt and black pepper. Lower the heat and simmer gently for 10 minutes.

2 Whisk the egg yolk in a small bowl until smooth. Stir a little hot sauce into yolk, then return the mixture to the saucepan. Cook over a low heat, stirring, for 30 seconds. Remove the pan from the heat and keep warm.

3 To make the lasagne. Heat the oil in a frying pan over a moderate heat and cook the garlic, stirring, until soft. Add the mushrooms to pan, increase the heat and cook, stirring, until golden. Stir in the herbs. Lower the heat and cook for 10 minutes or until the liquid almost evaporates. Remove from the heat and season with salt and pepper.

4 Preheat the oven. Line a buttered 20cm x 25cm/8in x 10in baking dish with $^1/_3$ of the pasta pieces, overlapping slightly. Spread with $^1/_3$ of the mushroom mixture, top with $^1/_3$ of the sauce and sprinkle with $^1/_3$ of the Parmesan. Repeat layers twice. Bake for 25–30 minutes or until bubbly and golden.

Serves 6
Preparation 35mins
Cooking 1hr
Calories 566
Fat 14g

Corn and Wild Rice Fritters with Tomato

**3 large vine ripened tomatoes,
cut into thick slices
2 cups rocket leaves**

Corn and Wild Rice Fritters
**2 cobs corn, kernels removed
1 cup cooked wild rice or wild
rice blend
1 tbsp chopped fresh parsley
1 tbsp snipped fresh chives
2 tsp fresh rosemary leaves,
chopped
2 eggs, lightly beaten
2 egg whites, lightly beaten
freshly ground black pepper**

1 To make the fritters. Heat a large nonstick frying pan over a high heat. Lightly spray or brush with unsaturated oil. Add the corn kernels. Cook, stirring, for 2–3 minutes or until they start to brown. Transfer to a large bowl. Add rice, parsley, chives, rosemary, eggs, egg whites and black pepper to taste. Mix to combine.

2 Lightly spray or brush frying pan with unsaturated oil. Place ¹/₂ cup of mixture in pan - allow room between each fritter for spreading. Cook for 2–3 minutes each side or until crisp and golden. Remove the fritters from the pan. Place on absorbent kitchen paper and keep warm while cooking the remaining mixture.

3 Meanwhile, preheat the grill to a high heat. Place the tomatoes on aluminium foil. Season with a pepper. Cook under the grill for 5 minutes or until hot. To serve, top each fritter with a few rocket leaves and some tomato slices.

Makes 6
Preparation 25mins
Cooking 15mins
Calories 173
Fat 2g

Tip: When cooking wild rice, to achieve beautiful plump grains with a curly appearance, place rice in cold water, bring to the boil and boil for 5 minutes. Turn off the heat, cover and steam for 20–30 minutes. Bring to the boil again and cook for 15 minutes longer or until the rice is tender.

Side Dishes

Some side dishes are so delicious, you have to keep yourself from swapping bowls. If you suffer from this complaint, we're sorry to say you'll find no help in these pages. Remoulade, tabbouleh, dauphinoise and olla gitana are particularly infectious bowl hogging conditions. Even old favorites like mash, marinated mushrooms and sweet and sour cabbage have been known to trigger episodes. The only treatment we can suggest is that you make some extra!

Potato and Onion Dauphinoise

OVEN TEMPERATURE
180°C, 350°F, GAS 4

Note: The cream slowly seeps into the layers of thinly sliced potato and onion in this wonderfully rich French gratin. Treat your friends to it on a special occasion.

**2 tsp butter, plus extra
for greasing
680g/1¹/₂ lb baking potatoes
3 onions, thinly sliced
salt and black pepper
1 tsp freshly grated nutmeg
2 cups light cream**

Serves 4
Preparation 15mins
Cooking 1hr
Calories 425
Fat 24g

1 Preheat the oven. Butter a shallow ovenproof dish. Thinly slice the potatoes using the slicing blade on a food processor, or with a sharp knife.
2 Arrange the potatoes and onions in alternate layers in the dish, lightly seasoning each layer with salt, pepper and nutmeg. Finish with a potato layer, then pour over the cream and dot with butter. Place on the lower shelf of the oven and cook for 1 hour or until golden brown

Photograph appears also on page 60

Corn Cobs with Mixed Vegetables in Coconut Milk

3–4 corn cobs
900g/2 lb mixed vegetables
(e.g. French beans, potatoes,
butternut pumpkin, carrot,
cauliflower, okra, etc)
$^1/_2$ bunch spinach
small bunch fresh coriander
2$^1/_2$ cm/1in piece fresh green
ginger
2 green chillies
2 tbsp oil
2 tsp salt
1 tsp each ground coriander and
cumin
1 cup coconut cream

3 Add the salt, ground coriander and cumin to the coconut cream and pour $^1/_2$ over the vegetables. Cover with a tight fitting lid and simmer very gently for 10–15 minutes or until vegetables are cooked but still crisp. Remove the lid and add the remaining coconut cream.

4 Serve immediately. Garnish with fresh coriander, if desired.

Serves 4–6
Preparation 25mins
Cooking 15mins
Calories 283
Fat 5g

1 Remove the outside leaves and as much silk as possible from the corn and cut each cob into 4 pieces. Peel and cut the mixed vegetables into chunks or cubes. Remove the white stalks and chop the spinach and coriander. Wash them both and set aside. Place the other vegetables in a colander and wash well. Peel and grate the ginger. Seed and chop the chillies.

2 Heat the oil in a large heavy saucepan. Add the ginger and chillies and stir in the corn pieces. Scatter over $^1/_2$ the chopped spinach and coriander, spoon in all the vegetables and scatter over the remaining spinach and coriander.

Celeriac and Herb Remoulade

2 medium eggs
455g/1 lb celeriac, grated
2 tbsp olive oil
1 tbsp sesame oil
juice of 1 lemon
3 tbsp chopped fresh parsley
3 tbsp snipped fresh chives
salt and black pepper

1 Bring a saucepan of water to the boil. Add the eggs and boil for 10 minutes. Cool under cold running water, then remove the shells and finely chop the eggs.

2 Place the celery root and chopped eggs in a large bowl. Mix together the olive oil, sesame oil and lemon juice and pour over the celery root and eggs. Add the parsley, chives and seasoning, then mix thoroughly.

Serves 4
Preparation 15mins
Cooking 10mins
Calories 161
Fat 14g

Summer Tabbouleh

6oz/170g bulgur wheat
2 medium eggs
1 red onion, finely chopped
2 cloves garlic, finely chopped
1 red and 1 yellow capsicum,
cored, deseeded and finely
chopped
1 tbsp each chopped fresh parsley,
chives and coriander
3 tbsp chopped fresh mint
grated zest and juice of 1 lemon
grated zest and juice of 1 lime
3 tbsp olive oil
salt and black pepper

1 Prepare the bulgur according to the packet instructions, until tender. Meanwhile, bring a saucepan of water to the boil. Add the eggs and boil for 10 minutes. Cool under cold running water, then remove the shells and mash the eggs.

2 Add the onion, garlic, capsicums, parsley, chives, coriander, mint, lemon and lime zest and juice, and the oil to the bulgur, then mix well. Season to taste before serving.

Note:
This Middle Eastern dish goes with almost anything. It's particularly good at buffets or barbecues. You can also serve it as a main course with a large salad.

Serves 4
Preparation 25mins
Cooking 10mins
Calories 220
Fat 15g

Orange-Glazed Cabbage

OVEN TEMPERATURE
200°C, 400°F, GAS 6

Note: This unusual but very simple glaze of marmalade, orange juice and maple syrup gives the cabbage a lovely sweetness. This dish is particularly good with sausages.

1 white cabbage, thinly sliced

Glaze
juice of 2 oranges
2 tbsp maple syrup
1 tbsp olive oil
3 tbsp marmalade
1 tsp salt

Serves 4
Preparation 10mins
Cooking 25mins
Calories 133
Fat 4g

1 Preheat the oven. To make the glaze, place the orange juice, syrup, oil and marmalade in a large bowl and stir. Season, add the cabbage and mix to coat thoroughly.
2 Remove the cabbage from the bowl, reserving the glaze, and spread out on a large baking tray. Pour over $1/2$ of the reserved glaze and cook for 15 minutes. Remove from the oven, toss the cabbage gently, then pour over the rest of the glaze. Return to the oven and bake for a further 10 minutes or until the cabbage has turned dark brown at the edges.

Spicy Cauliflower with Garlic

2 slices brown bread
1 cauliflower, cut into florets
salt and black pepper
4 tbsp olive oil
1 clove garlic, crushed
1 red chilli, finely chopped
8 black olives, pitted and halved
1 tbsp capers

1 Preheat the oven. Place the bread in the oven for 20 minutes or until it dries out and becomes crisp. Process in a food processor to make breadcrumbs. Alternatively, use a grater.

2 Place the cauliflower in a saucepan, cover with boiling water and add a little salt. Return to the boil, simmer for 1 minute or until slightly softened, then drain well.
3 Heat the oil in a large, heavy-based frying pan. Add the garlic, chilli and cauliflower and fry for 3 minutes or until the cauliflower starts to brown. Add the olives, capers, breadcrumbs and seasoning. Fry for a further 1 minute or until the breadcrumbs soak up the oil and flavourings.

Oven temperature
160°C, 325°F, Gas 3

Note:
This method of cooking cauliflower comes from Italy. The fantastic combination of Mediterranean flavours will revolutionise your attitude towards this humble vegetable.

Serves 4
Preparation 10mins
Cooking 25mins
Calories 201
Fat 16g

Potato and Parsley Croquettes

Note: Crisp and golden on the outside and meltingly soft inside, these croquettes are terribly moreish. They are especially good served with a dollop of tangy tomato relish.

Serves 4
Preparation 15mins + 1hr cooking
Cooking 40mins
Calories 434
Fat 27g

85g/3oz long-grain rice
2 large potatoes, cut into chunks
salt and black pepper
2 red onions, finely chopped
1 clove garlic, crushed
4 tbsp chopped fresh parsley
salt and pepper for seasoning
6 tbsp sesame seeds
sunflower oil for frying

1 Cook the rice according to the packet instructions, until tender, then drain well. Spread on a plate and leave for 1 hour or until cooled completely, fluffing it up with a fork occasionally.

2 Meanwhile, put the potatoes into a large saucepan of boiling salted water, then simmer for 15–20 minutes, until tender. Drain, then mash. Put the mashed potato into a large bowl with the cooled rice, onions, garlic, parsley and seasoning. Mix thoroughly.

3 Shape the mixture into 8 croquettes with your hands, then roll in the sesame seeds. Heat 1cm/$^1/_2$in of oil in a large, heavy-based frying pan and fry the croquettes for 2–3 minutes, turning until crisp and browned all over.

Sweet and Sour Red Cabbage

1 Preheat the oven. Put the oil, vinegar, chilli, orange zest and juice, orange-flower water and sugar into a small saucepan and simmer for 5 minutes.

2 Place the cabbage in an ovenproof casserole dish, then pour over the oil and vinegar mixture, reserving about 2 tablespoons. Cover with a lid or double layer of foil and bake for 3 hours, checking the cabbage every hour, and adding the remaining oil and vinegar mixture if it starts to dry out.

3 tbsp olive oil
2 tbsp red wine vinegar
1 red or green chilli, sliced, seeds and pith included
grated zest and juice of 1 orange
1 tbsp orange-flower water
3 tbsp light brown sugar
1 red cabbage, thinly sliced

Serves 4
Preparation 15mins
Cooking 3¼ hrs
Calories 196
Fat 11g

Oven temperature
160°C, 325°F, Gas 3

Note: Long, gentle cooking is essential for this dish, which is good either hot or cold. It goes particularly well with roast pork, venison and game birds such as pheasant.

Garlic and Potato Mash

Note: By gently frying garlic, you turn it from something really pungent into a sweet nutty flavouring. Add some to mashed potato and you'll get a pleasant surprise.

Serves 4
Preparation 15mins
Cooking 50mins
Calories 385
Fat 16g

1 kg/2¼ lb large potatoes, cut into chunks
3 tbsp olive oil
2 heads of garlic, cloves separated and peeled
1 red onion, chopped
3 tbsp crème fraîche
4 tbsp snipped fresh chives
salt and black pepper

1 Put the potatoes into a large saucepan of lightly salted boiling water, bring back to the boil, then simmer for 15–20 minutes, until tender.

2 Meanwhile, heat the oil in a -based frying pan or saucepan over a low to medium heat. Add the garlic cloves, cover the pan and cook gently for 10–15 minutes, until tender and golden at the edges. Remove the garlic and set aside. Add the onion to the oil and cook for 10 minutes or until softened.

3 Drain the potatoes, then return to the pan and add the garlic, onion and oil. Mash well, then stir in the crème fraîche and chives and season to taste.

Dijon Mushrooms

30g/1oz butter
4 pickling onions or shallots,
finely chopped
1 clove garlic, crushed
455g/1 lb mushrooms
¾ cup dry white wine
1 tbsp Dijon mustard
1 tsp finely chopped
fresh coriander
1¼ cups natural yoghurt
freshly ground black pepper
2 tbsp chopped fresh parsley

1 Melt the butter in a nonstick frying pan over a medium heat, add onions or shallots and garlic and cook, stirring, for 2–3 minutes or until onions or shallots are soft.
2 Add mushrooms and cook, stirring occasionally, for 5 minutes or until mushrooms are cooked. Remove mushrooms from pan, set aside and keep warm.
3 Stir wine, mustard and coriander into pan and bring to the boil. Reduce heat and simmer for 10 minutes or until liquid reduces by half. Remove pan from heat, stir in yoghurt and season to taste with black pepper. Return pan to a low heat, and cook for 2–3 minutes or until heated through. Spoon sauce over mushrooms, sprinkle with parsley and serve.

Serves 4
Preparation 10mins
Cooking 25mins
Calories 168
Fat 4.9g

Braised Witlof Gratin

Serves 4
Preparation 5mins
Cooking 25mins
Calories 291
Fat 24g

6 witlof or Belgium endive,
trimmed leaving root end intact,
halved lengthwise
1 tbsp fresh lemon juice
2 tbsp sweet butter, finely diced
$^1/_2$ tsp salt
2 tsp sugar
$^3/_4$ cup chicken stock
85g/3oz finely grated Gruyere
155g/5$^1/_2$oz dried breadcrumbs

1 Place the witlof, cut sides down, in two layers in a large, heavy based frying pan. Sprinkle with the lemon juice, butter, salt and sugar and add the stock.
2 Cover the witlof with a buttered round of greaseproof paper, then a lid, and bring to the boil. Lower the heat and simmer gently for 10 minutes or until the witlof is very tender.
3 Using a slotted spoon, transfer the witlof to a buttered gratin dish just large enough to hold them in a single layer. Combine the Gruyere and breadcrumbs and sprinkle evenly over the witlof.
4 Place the dish under a preheated moderate broiler for 3–4 minutes or until the cheese melts and the topping is golden. Serve hot.

Zucchini, Bean and Tomato Medley

Serves 4–6
Preparation 15mins
Cooking 20mins
Calories 135
Fat 1g

2 tbsp olive oil
1 large onion, sliced
1 clove garlic, crushed
1 tsp chopped fresh thyme or
oregano or $^1/_4$ tsp dried
pinch salt
freshly ground black pepper
455g/1 lb green beans, cut into
short lengths
455g/1 lb zucchinis, cut into
chunks
4 large tomatoes, quartered
55mL/2 fl oz/ water

1 Heat the oil in a large, heavy based frying pan over moderate heat and cook the onion and garlic, stirring, for 5–8 minutes or until the onion is golden. Stir in the thyme or oregano and season to taste with salt and pepper.
2 Add the green beans, zucchinis, tomatoes and water to the pan, mix lightly, cover and simmer gently for 10 minutes or until the vegetables are just tender.

Deep Fried Snake Beans

Serves 4–6
Preparation 15min
Cooking 5min
Calories 72
Fat >1g

2 cups vegetable oil for deep frying
455g/1 lb snake beans, cut into short lengths
1 tbsp finely chopped garlic
1 tbsp finely chopped fresh ginger
2 tbsp finely chopped spring onions
2 dried red chillies (optional)
1 tbsp Chinese rice wine or dry sherry
1 tbsp soy sauce
1 tbsp sugar
1 tbsp water

1 Heat the oil in a wok or a deep, heavy based frying pan until a single bean dropped in sizzles all over. Add $\frac{1}{2}$ the beans to pan and deep fry for 3–4 minutes or until slightly wrinkled. Using a slotted spoon, remove and drain on paper towels. Repeat with the remaining beans.

2 Remove the oil from the pan, wipe clean with paper towels and return to a high heat. Add 1 tablespoon of oil to the pan, add the garlic, ginger, spring onions and chillies (if using), and stir fry for 30 seconds or until the chillies blacken. Discard the chillies.

3 Add the wine or sherry, soy sauce, sugar and water to the pan and stir fry for 2–3 seconds. Return the beans to the pan, heat through and serve immediately.

Olla Gitana (Gypsy Stew)

2 medium sized eggplants
4 onions
2 green or red capsicums
2–3 cloves garlic
4 tomatoes
salt and black pepper
¹/₂ cup olive oil
¹/₂ cup black olives to garnish
¹/₂ cup chopped parsley to garnish

1 Cut the unpeeled eggplant into cubes, sprinkle with salt and leave for 1 hour. Rinse and pat dry with paper towels. Slice or quarter the onions and quarter the capsicums, removing the seeds and membranes. Chop the garlic and cut the tomatoes into thick slices.

2 In a medium sized saucepan, arrange in separate layers the onions, capsicums, garlic, eggplant and lastly the tomatoes, sprinkling each layer with salt and pepper to taste. Pour the oil over vegetables. Cover and simmer gently for 40 minutes. Serve topped with olives and parsley.

Serves 6
Preparation 15min
Cooking 40min
Calories 257
Fat 3g

Note: When buying vegetables for this dish look for tiny purple and white eggplant (smaller than a golf ball) baby fresh spring onions, bright red capsicums and small egg tomatoes. The vegetables are so young and tender they can be cooked whole (capsicums quartered).

Glossary

acidulated water: water with added acid, such as lemon juice or vinegar, which prevents discolouration of ingredients, particularly fruit or vegetables. The proportion of acid to water is 1 teaspoon per 300mL.

al dente: Italian cooking term for ingredients that are cooked until tender but still firm to the bite; usually applied to pasta.

americaine: method of serving seafood, usually lobster and monkfish, in a sauce flavoured with olive oil, aromatic herbs, tomatoes, white wine, fish stock, brandy and tarragon.

anglaise: cooking style for simple cooked dishes such as boiled vegetables. Assiette anglaise is a plate of cold cooked meats.

antipasto: Italian for 'before the meal', it denotes an assortment of cold meats, vegetables and cheeses, often marinated, served as an hors d'oeuvre. A typical antipasto might include salami, prosciutto, marinated artichoke hearts, anchovy fillets, olives, tuna fish and Provolone cheese.

au gratin: food sprinkled with breadcrumbs, often covered with cheese sauce and browned until a crisp coating forms.

balsamic vinegar: a mild, extremely fragrant, wine-based vinegar made in northern Italy. Traditionally, the vinegar is aged for at least seven years in a series of casks made of various woods.

baste: to moisten food while it is cooking by spooning or brushing on liquid or fat.

baine marie: a saucepan standing in a large pan which is filled with boiling water to keep liquids at simmering point. A double boiler will do the same job.

beat: to stir thoroughly and vigorously.

beurre manie: equal quantities of butter and flour kneaded together and added, a little at a time, to thicken a stew or casserole.

bird: see paupiette.

blanc: a cooking liquid made by adding flour and lemon juice to water in order to keep certain vegetables from discolouring as they cook.

blanch: to plunge into boiling water and then, in some cases, into cold water. Fruits and nuts are blanched to remove skin easily.

blanquette: a white stew of lamb, veal or chicken, bound with egg yolks and cream and accompanied by onion and mushrooms.

blend: to mix thoroughly.

bonne femme: dishes cooked in the traditional French 'housewife' style. Chicken and pork bonne femme are garnished with bacon, potatoes and baby onion; fish bonne femme with mushrooms in a white wine sauce.

bouquet garni: a bunch of herbs, usually consisting of sprigs of parsley, thyme, marjoram, rosemary, a bay leaf, peppercorns and cloves, tied in muslin and used to flavour stews and casseroles.

braise: to cook whole or large pieces of poultry, game, fish, meat or vegetables in a small amount of wine, stock or other liquid in a closed pot. Often the main ingredient is first browned in fat and then cooked in a low oven or very slowly on top of the stove. Braising suits tough meats and older birds and produces a mellow, rich sauce.

broil: the American term for grilling food.

brown: cook in a small amount of fat until brown.

burghul (also bulgur): a type of cracked wheat, where the kernels are steamed and dried before being crushed.

buttered: to spread with softened or melted butter.

butterfly: to slit a piece of food in half horizontally, cutting it almost through so that, when opened, it resembles butterfly wings. Chops, large prawns and thick fish fillets are often butterflied so that they cook more quickly.

buttermilk: a tangy, low-fat cultured milk product its slight acidity makes it an ideal marinade base for poultry.

calzone: a semicircular pocket of pizza dough, stuffed with meat or vegetables, sealed and baked.

caramelise: to melt sugar until it is a golden brown syrup.

champignons: small mushrooms, usually canned.

chasseur: (hunter) a French cooking style in which meat and chicken dishes are cooked with mushrooms, spring onions, white wine, and often tomato.

clarify: to melt butter and drain the oil off the sediment.

coat: to cover with a thin layer of flour, sugar, nuts, crumbs, poppy or sesame seeds, cinnamon sugar or a few of the ground spices.

concasser: to chop coarsely, usually tomatoes.

confit: from the French verb *confire*, meaning to preserve. Food that is made into a preserve by cooking very slowly and thoroughly until tender. In the case of meat, such as duck or goose, it is cooked in its own fat, and covered with the fat so that the meat does not come into contact with the air. Vegetables such as onions are good in confit.

consomme: a clear soup usually made from beef.

coulis: a thin puree, usually of fresh or cooked fruit or vegetables, which is soft enough to pour (couler means 'to run'). A coulis may be rough-textured or very smooth.

court bouillon: the liquid in which fish, poultry or meat is cooked. It usually consists of water with bay leaf, onion, carrots and salt and freshly ground black pepper to taste. Other additives may include wine, vinegar, stock, garlic or spring onions (scallions).

couscous: cereal processed from semolina into pellets, traditionally steamed and served with meat and vegetables in the classic North African stew of the same name.

cruciferous vegetables: certain members of the mustard, cabbage and turnip families with cross-shaped flowers and strong aromas and flavours.

cream: to make soft, smooth and creamy by rubbing with the back of a spoon or by beating with a mixer. Usually applied to fat and sugar.

croutons: small toasted or fried cubes of bread.

crudites: raw vegetables, cut in slices or sticks to nibble plain or with a dipping sauce, or shredded vegetables tossed as salad with a simple dressing.

cube: to cut into small pieces with six equal sides.

curdle: to cause milk or sauce to separate into solid and liquid. Example, overcooked egg mixtures.

daikon radish: (also called mooli): a long white Japanese radish.

dark sesame oil (also called Oriental sesame oil): dark polyunsaturated oil with a low burning point, used for seasoning. Do not replace with lighter sesame oil.

deglaze: to dissolve congealed cooking juices or glaze on the bottom of a pan by adding a liquid, then scraping and stirring vigorously whilst bringing the liquid to the boil. Juices may be used to make gravy or to add to sauce.

degrease: to skim grease from the surface of liquid. If possible the liquid should be chilled so the fat solidifies. If not, skim off most of the fat with a large metal spoon, then trail strips of paper towel on the surface of the liquid to remove any remaining globules.

devilled: a dish or sauce that is highly seasoned with a hot ingredient such as mustard, Worcestershire sauce or cayenne pepper.

dice: to cut into small cubes.

dietary fibre: a plant-cell material that is undigested or only partially digested in the human body, but which promotes healthy digestion of other food matter.

dissolve: mix a dry ingredient with liquid until absorbed.

dredge: to coat with a dry ingredient, as flour or sugar.

drizzle: to pour in a fine thread-like stream over a surface.

dust: to sprinkle or coat lightly with flour or icing sugar.

Dutch oven: a heavy casserole with a lid usually made from cast iron or pottery.

emulsion: a mixture of two liquids that are not mutually soluble- for example, oil and water.

entree: in Europe, the 'entry' or hors d'oeuvre; in North America entree means the main course.

fillet: special cut of beef, lamb, pork or veal; breast of poultry and game; fish cut off the bone lengthways.

flake: to break into small pieces with a fork.

flame: to ignite warmed alcohol over food.

fold in: a gentle, careful combining of a light or delicate mixture with a heavier mixture, using a metal spoon.

fricassee: a dish in which poultry, fish or vegetables are bound together with a white or veloute sauce. In Britain and the United States, the name applies to an old-fashioned dish of chicken in a creamy sauce.

galette: sweet or savoury mixture shaped as a flat round.

garnish: to decorate food, usually with something edible.

gastrique: caramelized sugar deglazed with vinegar and used in fruit-flavoured savoury sauces, in such dishes as duck with orange.

glaze: a thin coating of beaten egg, syrup or aspic which is brushed over pastry, fruits or cooked meats.

gluten: a protein in flour that is developed when dough is kneaded, making the dough elastic.

gratin: a dish cooked in the oven or under the grill so that it develops a brown crust. Breadcrumbs or cheese may be sprinkled on top first. Shallow gratin dishes ensure a maximum area of crust.

grease: to rub or brush lightly with oil or fat.

joint: to cut poultry, game or small animals into serving pieces by dividing at the joint.

julienne: to cut food into match-like strips.

knead: to work dough using heel of hand with a pressing motion, while stretching and folding the dough.

line: to cover the inside of a container with paper, to protect or aid in removing mixture.

infuse: to immerse herbs, spices or other flavourings in hot liquid to flavour it. Infusion takes from 2-5 minutes depending on the flavouring. The liquid should be very hot but not boiling.

jardiniere: a garnish of garden vegetables, typically carrots, pickling onions, French beans and turnips.

lights: lungs of an animal, used in various meat preparations such as pâtés and faggots.

macerate: to soak food in liquid to soften.

marinade: a seasoned liquid, usually an oil and acid mixture, in which meats or other foods are soaked to soften and give more flavour.

marinara: Italian 'sailor's style' cooking that does not apply to any particular combination of ingredients. Marinara tomato sauce for pasta is the most familiar.

marinate: to let food stand in a marinade to season and tenderise.

mask: to cover cooked food with sauce.

melt: to heat until liquified.

mince: to grind into very small pieces.

mix: to combine ingredients by stirring.

monounsaturated fats: one of three types of fats found in foods. Are believed not to raise the level of cholesterol in the blood.

nicoise: a garnish of tomatoes, garlic and black olives; a salad with anchovy, tuna and French beans is typical.

non-reactive pan: a cooking pan whose surface does not chemically react with food. Materials used include stainless steel, enamel, glass and some alloys.

noisette: small 'nut' of lamb cut from boned loin or rack that is rolled, tied and cut in neat slices. Noisette also means flavoured with hazelnuts, or butter cooked to a nut brown colour.

normande: a cooking style for fish, with a garnish of prawn, mussels and mushrooms in a white wine cream sauce; for poultry and meat, a sauce with cream, calvados and apple.

olive oil: various grades of oil extracted from olives. Extra virgin olive oil has a full, fruity flavour and the lowest acidity. Virgin olive oil is slightly higher in acidity and lighter in flavour. Pure olive oil is a processed blend of olive oils and has the highest acidity and lightest taste.

panade: a mixture for binding stuffings and dumplings, notably quenelles, often of choux pastry or simply breadcrumbs. A panade may also be made of frangipane, pureed potatoes or rice.

papillote: to cook food in oiled or buttered greaseproof paper or aluminum foil. Also a decorative frill to cover bone ends of chops and poultry drumsticks.

parboil: to boil or simmer until part cooked (i.e. cooked further than when blanching).

pare: to cut away outside covering.

pate: a paste of meat or seafood used as a spread for toast or crackers.

paupiette: a thin slice of meat, poultry or fish spread with a savoury stuffing and rolled. In the United States this is also called 'bird' and in Britain an 'olive'.

peel: to strip away outside covering.

plump: to soak in liquid or moisten thoroughly until full and round.

poach: to simmer gently in enough hot liquid to cover, using care to retain shape of food.

polyunsaturated fat: one of the three types of fats found in food. These exist in large quantities in such vegetable oils as safflower, sunflower, corn and soya bean. These fats lower the level of cholesterol in the blood.

puree: a smooth paste, usually of vegetables or fruits, made by putting foods through a sieve, food mill or liquefying in a blender or food processor.

ragout: traditionally a well seasoned, rich stew containing meat, vegetables and wine. Nowadays, a term applied to any stewed mixture.

ramekins: small oval or round individual baking dishes.

reconstitute: to put moisture back into dehydrated foods by soaking in liquid.

reduce: to cook over a very high heat, uncovered, until the liquid is reduced by evaporation.

refresh: to cool hot food quickly, either under running water or by plunging it into iced water, to stop it cooking. Particularly for

vegetables and occasionally for shellfish.

rice vinegar: mild, fragrant vinegar that is less sweet than cider vinegar and not as harsh as distilled malt vinegar. Japanese rice vinegar is milder than the Chinese variety.

roulade: a piece of meat, usually pork or veal, that is spread with stuffing, rolled and often braised or poached. A roulade may also be a sweet or savoury mixture that is baked in a Swiss roll tin or paper case, filled with a contrasting filling, and rolled.

rubbing-in: a method of incorporating fat into flour, by use of fingertips only. Also incorporates air into mixture.

safflower oil: the vegetable oil that contains the highest proportion of polyunsaturated fats.

salsa: a juice derived from the main ingredient being cooked, or a sauce added to a dish to enhance its flavour. In Italy the term is often used for pasta sauces; in Mexico the name usually applies to uncooked sauces served as an accompaniment, especially to corn chips.

saturated fats: one of the three types of fats found in foods. These exist in large quantities in animal products, coconut and palm oils; they raise the level of cholesterol in the blood. As high cholesterol levels may cause heart disease, saturated fat consumption is recommended to be less than 15 percent of calories provided by the daily diet.

sauté: to cook or brown in small amount of hot fat.

score: to mark food with cuts, notches or lines to prevent curling or to make food more attractive.

scald: to bring just to boiling point, usually for milk. Also to rinse with boiling water.

sear: to brown surface quickly over high heat in hot dish.

seasoned flour: flour with salt and pepper added.

sift: to shake a dry, powdered substance through a sieve or sifter to remove any lumps and give lightness.

simmer: to cook food gently in liquid that bubbles steadily just below boiling point so that the food cooks in even heat without breaking up.

singe: to quickly flame poultry to remove all traces of feathers after plucking.

skim: to remove a surface layer (often of impurities and scum) from a liquid with a metal spoon or small ladle.

slivered: sliced in long, thin pieces, usually refers to nuts, especially almonds.

soften: example: gelatine - sprinkle over cold water and allow to gel (soften) then dissolve and liquefy.

souse: to cover food, particularly fish, in wine vinegar and spices and cook slowly; the food is cooled in the same liquid. Sousing gives food a pickled flavour.

steep: to soak in warm or cold liquid in order to soften food and draw out strong flavours or impurities.

stir-fry: to cook thin slices of meat and vegetable over a high heat in a small amount of oil, stirring constantly to even cooking in a short time. Traditionally cooked in a wok, however a heavy-based frying pan may be used.

stock: a liquid containing flavours, extracts and nutrients of bones, meat, fish or vegetables.

stud: to adorn with; for example, baked ham studded with whole cloves.

sweat: to cook vegetables over heat until only juices run.

sugo: an Italian sauce made from the liquid or juice extracted from fruit or meat during cooking.

sweat: to cook sliced or chopped food, usually vegetables, in a little fat and no liquid over very low heat. Foil is pressed on top so that the food steams in its own juices, usually before being added to other dishes.

timbale: a creamy mixture of vegetables or meat baked in a mould. French for 'kettledrum'; also denotes a drum-shaped baking dish.

thicken: to make a thin, smooth paste by mixing together arrowroot, cornflour or flour with an equal amount of cold water; stir into hot liquid, cook, stirring until thickened.

toss: to gently mix ingredients with two forks or fork and spoon.

total fat: the individual daily intake of all three fats previously described in this glossary. Nutritionists recommend that fats provide no more than 35percent of the energy in the diet.

vine leaves: tender, lightly flavoured leaves of the grapevine, used in ethnic cuisine as wrappers for savoury mixtures. As the leaves are usually packed in brine, they should be well rinsed before use.

whip: to beat rapidly, incorporate air and produce expansion.

zest: thin outer layer of citrus fruits containing the aromatic citrus oil. It is usually thinly pared with a vegetable peeler, or grated with a zester or grater to separate it from the bitter white pith underneath.

Weights and Measures

Cooking is not an exact science; one does not require finely calibrated scales, pipettes and scientific equipment to cook, yet the conversion to metric measures in some countries and its interpretations must have intimidated many a good cook.

In the recipes weights are given for ingredients such as meats, fish, poultry and some vegetables, but in normal cooking a few ounces or grams one way or another will not affect the success of your dish.

Allthough recipes have been tested using the Australian Standard 250mL cup, 20mL tablespoon and 5mL teaspoon, they will work just as well with the US and Canadian 8fl oz cup, or the UK 300mL cup. We have used graduated cup measures in preference to tablespoon measures so that proportions are always the same. Where tablespoon measures have been given, they are not crucial measures, so using the smaller tablespoon of the US or UK will not affect the recipe's success. At least we all agree on the teaspoon size.

For breads, cakes and pastries, the only area which might cause concern is where eggs are used, as proportions will then vary. If working with a 250mL or 300mL cup, use large eggs (65g/2$^{1}/_{4}$oz), adding a little more liquid to the recipe for 300mL cup measures if it seems necessary. Use the medium-sized eggs (55g/2oz) with 8fl oz cup measure. A graduated set of measuring cups and spoons is recommended, the cups in particular for measuring dry ingredients. Remember to level such ingredients to ensure an accurate quantity.

English Measures

All measurements are similar to Australian with two exceptions: the English cup measures 300mL/10$^{1}/_{2}$fl oz, whereas the American and Australian cup measure 250mL/8$^{3}/_{4}$ fl oz. The English tablespoon (the Australian dessertspoon) measures 14.8mL /1$^{1}/_{2}$ fl oz against Australian tablespoon of 20mL/$^{3}/_{4}$ fl oz. The Imperial measurement is 20fl oz to the pint, 40fl oz a quart and 160fl oz one gallon.

American Measures

The American reputed pint is 16fl oz, a quart is equal to 32fl oz and the American gallon, 128fl oz. The American tablespoon is equal to 14.8mL/$^{1}/_{2}$fl oz, the teaspoon is 5mL/$^{1}/_{6}$fl oz. The cup measure is 250 mL/8$^{3}/_{4}$ fl oz.

Dry Measures

All the measures are level, so when you have filled a cup or spoon, level it off with the edge of a knife. The scale below is the 'cook's equivalent'; it is not an exact conversion of metric to imperial measurement. To calculate the exact metric equivalent yourself, multiply onces x 28.349523 to obtain grams, or divide 28.349523 grams to obtain onces.

Metric	Imperial
g = grams	oz = ounces
kg = kilograms	lb = pound
15g	$^{1}/_{2}$oz
20g	$^{2}/_{3}$oz
30g	1oz
55g	2oz
85g	3oz
115g	4oz/$^{1}/_{4}$ lb
125g	4$^{1}/_{2}$oz
140/145g	5oz
170g	6oz
200g	7oz
225g	8oz/$^{1}/_{2}$ lb
315g	11oz
340g	12oz/$^{3}/_{4}$ lb
370g	13oz
400g	14oz
425g	15oz
455g	16oz/1 lb
1,000g/1kg	35.3oz/2.2 lb
1.5kg	3.33 lb

Oven Temperatures

The Celsius temperatures given here are not exact; they have been rounded off and are given as a guide only. Follow the manufacturer's temperature guide, relating it to oven description given in the recipe. Remember gas ovens are hottest at the top, electric ovens at the bottom and convection-fan forced ovens are usually even throughout. We included Regulo numbers for gas cookers which may assist. To convert °C to °F multiply °C by 9 and divide by 5 then add 32.

Oven Temperatures

	C°	F°	Gas regulo
Very slow	120	250	1
Slow	150	300	2
Moderately slow	160	325	3
Moderate	180	350	4
Moderately hot	190–200	370–400	5–6
Hot	210–220	410–440	6–7
Very hot	230	450	8
Super hot	250–290	475–500	9–10

Cake Dish Sizes

metric	imperial
15cm	6in
18cm	7in
20cm	8in
23cm	9in

Loaf Dish Sizes

metric	imperial
23 x 12cm	9 x 5in
25 x 8cm	10 x 3in
28 x 18cm	11 x 7in

Liquid Measures

metric	imperial	cup and spoon
mL	fl oz	
millilitres	fluid ounce	
5mL	$^1/_6$ fl oz	1 teaspoon
20mL	$^2/_3$ fl oz	1 tablespoon
30mL	1 fl oz	1 tbsp + 2 tsp
55mL	2 fl oz	
63mL	$2^1/_4$ fl oz	$^1/_4$ cup
85mL	3 fl oz	
115mL	4 fl oz	
125mL	$4^1/_2$ fl oz	$^1/_2$ cup
150mL	$5^1/_4$ fl oz	
188mL	$6^2/_3$ fl oz	$^3/_4$ cup
225mL	8 fl oz	
250mL	$8^3/_4$ fl oz	1 cup
300mL	$10^1/_2$ fl oz	
370mL	13 fl oz	
400mL	14 fl oz	
438mL	$15^1/_2$ fl oz	$1^3/_4$ cups
455mL	16 fl oz	
500mL	$17^1/_2$ fl oz	2 cups
570mL	20 fl oz	
1 litre	35.3 fl oz	4 cups

Cup Measurements

One cup is equal to the following weights.

	Metric	Imperial
Almonds, flaked	85g	3oz
Almonds, slivered, ground	125g	$4^1/_2$ oz
Almonds, kernel	155g	$5^1/_2$ oz
Apples, dried, chopped	125g	$4^1/_2$ oz

	Metric	Imperial
Apricots, dried, chopped	190g	$6^3/_4$ oz
Breadcrumbs, packet	125g	$4^1/_2$ oz
Breadcrumbs, soft	55g	2oz
Cheese, grated	115g	4oz
Choc bits	$155^1/_2$ g	5oz
Coconut, desiccated	90g	3oz
Cornflakes	30g	1oz
Currants	$155^1/_2$ g	5oz
Flour	115g	4oz
Fruit, dried (mixed, sultanas etc)	170g	6 oz
Ginger, crystallised, glace	250g	8oz
Honey, treacle, golden syrup	315g	11oz
Mixed peel	225g	8oz
Nuts, chopped	115g	4oz
Prunes, chopped	225g	8oz
Rice, cooked	155g	$5^1/_2$ oz
Rice, uncooked	225g	8oz
Rolled oats	90g	3oz
Sesame seeds	115g	4oz
Shortening (butter, margarine)	225g	8oz
Sugar, brown	155g	$5^1/_2$ oz
Sugar, granulated or caster	225g	8oz
Sugar, sifted icing	155g	$5^1/_2$ oz
Wheatgerm	60g	2oz

Length

Some of us still have trouble converting imperial length to metric. In this scale, measures have been rounded off to the easiest-to-use and most acceptable figures. To obtain the exact metric equivalent in converting inches to centimetres, multiply inches by 2.54 whereby 1 inch equals 25.4 millimetres and 1 millimetre equals 0.03937 inches.

Metric	Imperial
mm=millimetres	in = inches
cm=centimetres	ft = feet
5mm, 0.5cm	$^1/_4$ in
10mm, 1.0cm	$^1/_2$ in
20mm, 2.0cm	$^3/_4$ in
2.5cm	1in
5 cm	2in
$7^1/_2$ cm	3in
10cm	4in
$12^1/_2$ cm	5in
15cm	6in
18cm	7in
20cm	8in
23cm	9in
25cm	10in
28cm	11in
30cm	12in, 1 foot

Index